Oxford International Lower Secondary

9

English
Student Book

Eve Sullivan
Rachel Redford

OXFORD

OXFORD
UNIVERSITY PRESS

Great Clarendon Street, Oxford, OX2 6DP, United Kingdom

Oxford University Press is a department of the University of Oxford.
It furthers the University's objective of excellence in research, scholarship, and education by publishing worldwide. Oxford is a registered trade mark of Oxford University Press in the UK and in certain other countries.

© Oxford University Press 2023

The moral rights of the authors have been asserted.

First published in 2023

All rights reserved. No part of this publication may be reproduced, stored in a retrieval system, or transmitted, in any form or by any means, without the prior permission in writing of Oxford University Press, or as expressly permitted by law, by licence or under terms agreed with the appropriate reprographics rights organization. Enquiries concerning reproduction outside the scope of the above should be sent to the Rights Department, Oxford University Press, at the address above.

You must not circulate this work in any other form and you must impose this same condition on any acquirer

British Library Cataloguing in Publication Data

Data available

ISBN 978-1-38-203601-6

10 9 8 7 6 5 4 3 2 1

The manufacturing process conforms to the environmental regulations of the country of origin.

Printed in the UK
by Bell and Bain Ltd, Glasgow

FSC www.fsc.org MIX Paper | Supporting responsible forestry FSC® C007785

Acknowledgements

The publisher and authors would like to thank the following for permission to use photographs and other copyright material:

Cover: Dan Gartman. **Photos: p5:** Mireya Acierto/Getty Images; **p7(t):** Rawpixel.com/Shutterstock; **p7(b):** Halfpoint/Shutterstock; **p8:** North Wind Picture Archives / Alamy Stock Photo; **p9:** ArchMan/Shutterstock; **p11(t):** Tom Wang/Shutterstock; **p11(b):** Motortion Films/Shutterstock; **p12(t):** Amos Morgan/Getty Images; **p12(m):** Sorapop Udomsri/Shutterstock; **p12(b):** NakoPhotography; **p13(t):** Kent Weakley/Shuttterstock; **p13(b):** Vladimir V. Georgievskiy/Shutterstock; **p14:** Jodie Griggs/Getty Images; **p15:** Belinda Howell/Getty Images; **p17:** TCD/Prod.DB / Alamy Stock Photo; **p19:** rangizzz/Shutterstock; **p20:** PictureLux / The Hollywood Archive / Alamy Stock Photo; **p22(t):** A. Blanke/Shutterstock; **p22(b):** sdecoret/Shutterstock; **p23:** Chronicle / Alamy Stock Photo; **p24:** AF archive / Alamy Stock Photo; **p27(t):** Pictorial Press Ltd / Alamy Stock Photo; **p27(b):** BGSmith/Shutterstock; **p30:** pio3/Shutterstock; **p32(tl):** incamerastock / Alamy Stock Photo; **p32(tr):** ERIK STRODL / Alamy Stock Photo; **p32(bl):** Bill Waterson / Alamy Stock Photo; **p32(br):** Shawshots / Alamy Stock Photo; **p33(tl):** michaeljung/Shutterstock; **p33(tr):** Iryna Rasko/Shutterstock; **p33(b):** Antonio Salaverry/Shutterstock; **p34:** myphotobank.com.au/Shutterstock; **p36:** Romolo Tavani/Shutterstock; **p39:** M.Aurelius/Shutterstock; **p41:** Splash News; **p42:** Lynne Sladky/AP/Shutterstock; **p43:** Matthew Jacques/Shutterstock; **p44:** Sunshine Seeds/Shutterstock; **p45:** JJ pixs/Shutterstock; **p46(t):** Douglas Freer/Shutterstock; **p46(b):** Moviestore Collection Ltd / Alamy Stock Photo; **p47:** Donald Cooper / Alamy Stock Photo; **p49:** Jeff Gilbert / Alamy Stock Photo; **p50:** Neil Austen/Getty Images; **p51:** REUTERS / Alamy Stock Photo; **p52:** CARL DE SOUZA/AFP via Getty Images; **p53:** Album / Alamy Stock Photo; **p55:** Allan Cash Picture Library / Alamy Stock Photo; **p57(t):** BearFotos/Shutterstock **p57(b):** Andrey_Popov/Shutterstock; **p58:** snvv18870020330/Shutterstock; **p59:** Burke/Triolo Productions/Getty Images; **p61:** Caia Image/Getty Images; **p63:** Jag_cz/Shutterstock; **p64(tl):** Stockbyte/Getty Images; **p64(tr):** Monkey Business Images/Shutterstock; **p64(bl):** Monkey Business Images/Shutterstock; **p64(br):** michaeljung/Shutterstock; **p65:** Tom Arne Hanslien / Alamy Stock Photo; **p66:** Chronicle / Alamy Stock Photo; **p68:** Edwin Remsberg / Alamy Stock Photo; **p69:** Chronicle / Alamy Stock Photo; **p71:** Alpha Stock / Alamy Stock Photo; **p72:** Jeoffrey Maitem/Getty Images; **p73(t):** Milju varghese/Shutterstock; **p73(b):** Ed Connor/Shutterstock; **p74:** TonNam50/Shutterstock; **p75:** Chantal de Bruijne/Shutterstock; **p76:** Claudio Rampinini/Shutterstock; **p78:** fotoarek / Shutterstock; **p79:** PaoloBruschi/Shutterstock; **p80:** Nejron Photo/Shutterstock; **p81:** Fine Art Images/Heritage Images/Getty Images; **p82:** Stocksnapper/Shutterstock; **p83:** Daniel Wiedemann/Shutterstock; **p84:** Patrick McCabe / Alamy Stock Photo; **p86:** Sonifo/iStock/Getty Images; **p87(t):** Suman Kumar / Alamy Stock Photo; **p87(b):** FiledIMAGE/Shutterstock; **p88:** Net Vector/Shutterstock; **p89:** Victor Tyakht/Shutterstock; **p91:** Sorapong Chaipanya/Shutterstock; **p92:** adrian arbib / Alamy Stock Photo; **p94:** Jack Vartoogian/Getty Images; **p96:** Debbie Ann Powell/Shutterstock; **p97:** Reading Room 2020 / Alamy Stock Photo; **p101:** Rebecca Anne/Shutterstock; **p103:** robwatership / Alamy Stock Photo; **p104:** William Booth/Shutterstock; **p105:** Jacob_09/Shutterstock; **p106:** AFP / Getty Images; **p107:** Pictorial Press Ltd / Alamy Stock Photo; **p108:** REUTERS / Alamy Stock Photo; **p109:** Robyn Mackenzie/Shutterstock; **p110:** Romaine W/Shutterstock; **p111:** Retro AdArchives / Alamy Stock Photo; **p113:** Spectral-Design / Shutterstock; **p115:** Sarah Holmlund/Shutterstock; **p117:** serjoe / Shutterstock; **p119:** PA Images / Alamy Stock Photo; **p120(t):** Monkey Business Images/Shutterstock; **p120(m):** Ben Gingell/Shutterstock; **p120(bl):** Vlad-Koarov/Etoon.com; **p120(br):** 3000ad/Shutterstock; **p121(t):** St. Nick / Shutterstock; **p121(b):** Salienko Evgenii/Shutterstock; **p122:** Jesus Cobaleda/Shutterstock; **p123:** INTERFOTO / Alamy Stock Photo; **p124:** Netfalls Remy Musser / Shutterstock; **p125:** incamerastock / Alamy Stock Photo; **p126:** Andrew Fox / Alamy Stock Photo; **p127(t):** Public Domain; **p127(bl):** Svintage Archive / Alamy Stock Photo; **p127(br):** Keith Corrigan / Alamy Stock Photo; **p128:** Daniel Hebert / Shutterstock; **p129(l):** Pictorial Press Ltd / Alamy Stock Photo; **p129(r):** Pictorial Press Ltd / Alamy Stock Photo; **p130:** Igor Kolos / Shutterstock; **p132:** Reuters/Suhaib Salem; **p133:** Diane Diederich/Shutterstock; **p135(t):** monticello/Shutterstock; **p135(b):** Farizun Amrod Saad/Shutterstock; **p139:** GRANGER - Historical Picture Archive / Alamy Stock Photo; **p140:** CPA Media Pte Ltd / Alamy Stock Photo; **p141:** Southampton City Art Gallery / Bridgeman Images; **p143:** akg-images / Suzanne Held; **p145:** Photo © Bonhams, London, UK / Bridgeman Images; **p146:** imageBROKER / Alamy Stock Photo; **p147:** BGStock72/Shutterstock; **p148(t):** Sean Pavone/Shutterstock; **p148(bl):** sharptoyou/Shutterstock; **p148(br):** Pictorial Press Ltd / Alamy Stock Photo; **p149:** Abraham_stockero/Shutterstock; **p149(inset):** mark reinstein/Shutterstock; **p150:** Michele D'Ottavio / Alamy Stock Photo; **p151:** Ryan Rodrick Beiler/Shutterstock; **p152:** Redorbital Photography / Alamy Stock Photo; **p153:** A. C. Shelton/ClassicStock/Getty Images; **p154:** Hulton Archive / Stringer/Getty Images; **p156:** EDUARDO MUNOZ ALVAREZ/AFP via Getty Images; **p157:** BlurryMe/Shutterstock; **p158:** GRANGER - Historical Picture Archvie / Alamy Stock Photo; **p162(t):** Pakhnyushcha / Shutterstock; **p162(b):** Inspiration GP/Shutterstock; **p163:** Yuri Arcurs/Dreamstime; **p165:** Dogora Sun/Shutterstock; **p167:** Howard Davies/CORBIS/Corbis via Getty Images; **p168(t):** miwa-in-oz/Shutterstock; **p168(b):** tarapong srichaiyos/Shutterstock; **p171:** Darling Archive / Alamy Stock Photo; **p172:** John Birdsall Social Issues Photo Library / Science Photo Library; **p173:** Sean Pavone/Shutterstock; **p174:** LianeM / Shutterstock; **p175:** Sue Martin/Shutterstock; **p177:** © Sara Hayward. All Rights Reserved 2022 / Bridgeman Images; **p178(bkg):** New Africa/Shutterstock; **p178(l):** Freebird7977/Shutterstock; **p178(m):** AYO Production/Shutterstock; **p178(r):** Eteri Okrochelidze/Shutterstock; **p180:** Five/Getty Images; **p181:** wavebreakmedia/Shutterstock; **p182(t):** AlessandroBiascioli/Shutterstock; **p182(b):** Shyamalamuralinath/Shutterstock; **p183:** MFAHEEM FAHEEM/Shutterstock; **p184:** Saleem Ahmad Sheikh/Shutterstock; **p185(t):** Tinseltown/Shutterstock; **p185(b):** Chaosamran_Studio/Shutterstock; **p187:** Textile Value Chain; **p189:** Historic Images / Alamy Stock Photo; **p191(t):** Antiquarian Images / Alamy Stock Photo; **p191(b):** Dragon Images/Shutterstock.

Artwork by Dan Gartman, and Q2A Media.

Richard Adams: extract from *Watership Down* (Puffin, 2007), reprinted by permission of David Higham Associates Ltd.

Allan Ahlberg: extract from 'Billy McBone' from *Heard It in the Playground* (Viking, 1989), copyright © Allan Ahlberg 1989, reprinted by permission of Penguin Books Ltd.

Moniza Alvi: 'Presents From My Aunts in Pakistan', published by Bloodaxe Books. Reprinted by permission of publishers.

Ethan Ames: extract from interview with Georgie Henley and James McAvoy as posted on CineCon site on 12 August 2005, www.cinecon.com, reprinted by permission of United Agents.

Isaac Asimov: extract from 'Reason' in *I, Robot* (HarperCollins, 1993) first published 1950, reprinted by permission of Random House Inc.

Clare Atkins: extract from *Nona and Me* (Black Inc Books, 2016), reprinted by permission of the publishers.

Leo Benedictus: extract from 'Sky High: The Air Traffic Controller' printed in The Guardian 18.10.2008, reprinted by permission of Guardian News and Media.

Alan Bennett: extracts from Act 1 of *The History Boys* (Faber, 2004), reprinted by permission of Faber and Faber Ltd and United Agents.

John Berendt: opening extract from *The City of Falling Angels* (Hodder & Stoughton, 2005), reprinted by permission of the publishers of PLS Clear.

James Berry: extract from 'Old Slave Villages' from *Windrush Songs* (Bloodaxe, 2007), reprinted by permission of Bloodaxe Books.

Alain de Botton: extract from *The School of Life*, Hamish Hamilton; 1st edition (5 Sept. 2019); Penguin Random House, (3 Sept 2020), reprinted by permission of Penguin Random House.

Anthony Bourdain: extract from *Kitchen Confidential* (Bloomsbury, 2000), reprinted by permission of Bloomsbury USA.

E.R. Braithwaite: extract from *To Sir with Love* (Vintage, 2005), reprinted by permission of David Higham Associates Ltd.

Rachel Carson: *Silent Spring* originally serialized in *The New Yorker* magazine; first published September 27, 1962 (Houghton Mifflin Harcourt), reprinted by permission of Frances Collins.

Arthur C. Clarke: extract from *A Fall of Moondust* Gollancz, 2012 copyright © Arthur C Clarke 1961 reprinted with permission of David Higham Associates.

Michael Clerizo: 'Airport tourism' by Michael Clerizo from *The Lonely Planet Guide to Experimental Travel* edited by Rachael Antony and Joel Henry, reprinted by permission of Michael Clerizo.

Gaye Hicyilmaz: extract from *Against the Storm* (Faber, 1998), reprinted by permission of Faber and Faber Ltd.

Khaled Hosseini: extract from *The Kite Runner* (Bloomsbury, 2003), reprinted by permission of the publisher, Penguin Group USA.

Langston Hughes: 'I Too Sing America' from *The Collected Poems of Langston Hughes* edited by Arnold Rampersad (Alfred Knopf, 2007), reprinted by permission of David Higham Associates Ltd.

Holbrook Jackson: 'Town', first published in 1913, from *Occasions: A Volume of Essays upon Divers Subjects* (Grant Richards Ltd, 1922), reprinted by permission of The Society of Authors as the Literary Representative of the Estate of Holbrook Jackson.

Elizabeth Jennings: 'Friends' from *New Collected Poems* edited by Michael Schmidt (Carcanet, 2002), reprinted by permission of David Higham Associates Ltd.

Kathy Jetñil-Kijiner: Extract from poem 'Dear Matafele Peinam', in *Iep Jaltok: Poems from a Marshallese Daughter* by Kathy Jetñil-Kijiner, University of Arizona Press (2017). Reprinted by permission of publisher.

Brian Jones: 'About Friends' from *Spitfire on the Northern Line* (Chatto & Windus, 1975), reprinted by permission of The Random House Group Ltd.

Mohja Kahf: 'The Roc' from *The Poetry of Arab Women: A Contemporary Anthology* edited by Nathalie Handal (Interlink Books, 2001), reprinted by permission of the author.

Martin Luther King Jr: extracts from 'I Have a Dream...', copyright © 1963 Martin Luther King Jr, copyright renewed 1991 by Coretta Scott King, reprinted by arrangement with the heirs of the Estate of Martin Luther King Jr, c/o Writers House as agent for the Proprietor, New York, NY.

Kevin Kwan: extract from *Rich People Problems* (Knopf, 2017), reprinted with permission of Penguin Random House Ltd.

Tanya Landman: *Lightning Strike* © Tanya Landman 2021, reprinted with permission of author.

C.S. Lewis: extract from *The Lion, the Witch and the Wardrobe* (Meeting Mr Tumnus) (HarperCollins Childrens' Books, 2007), copyright © C S Lewis Pte Ltd 1950, reprinted by permission of The CS Lewis Company.

Bonnie Malkin: extract from 'American tourist clings to train through Australian outback' published in *Daily Telegraph*, Sydney. Reprinted by permission of publisher.

Nelson Mandela: extract from *A Long Walk to Freedom* (Little, Brown, 1994), copyright © Nelson Rolihlahla Mandela 1994, reprinted by permission of the publishers, Little, Brown Book Group via PLS Clear.

Vesna Maric: extract from *Bluebird: A Memoir* (Granta, 2009), reprinted by permission of the publishers, Granta Books.

Patricia McCormick: extract from 'If only Papa hadn't Danced' from *Stories Celebrating Human Rights* (Walker Books for Amnesty International, 2009), reprinted by permission of author.

Adrian Mitchell: extract from 'Secret Country' from *Love Songs of World War Three* (Allison & Busby, 1989), reprinted by permission of United Agents on behalf of the author's estate.

An Na: extract from *A Step from Heaven* (Allen & Unwin, 2002), reprinted by permission of Simon and Schuster.

George Orwell: extract from *Down and Out in Paris and London* (first published 1933), copyright © George Orwell 1933, renewed 1961 by Sonia Pitt-Rivers, reprinted by permission of Penguin Random House Ltd.

Orhan Pamuk: extract from *Istanbul: Memories of a City* translated by Maureen Freely (Faber, 2005), reprinted by permission of Faber and Faber Ltd.

Alice Pung: extract from *Unpolished Gem* (Portobello, 2008), and *Lucy and Linh* (Knopf, 2014) copyright © Alice Pung, reprinted by permission of Black Inc. Books Australia and Penguin Group USA.

Antoine de Saint-Exupéry: extract from *Southern Mail* translated by Curtis Cate (Penguin, 2000), reprinted by permission of The Random House Group Ltd.

Carl Sandburg: 'Fog' from *The Complete Poems of Carl Sandburg* (Houghton Mifflin, 2003), reprinted by permission of HarperCollins.

Marin Sorescu: 'Playing Icarus' from *The Biggest Egg in the World* (Bloodaxe, 1987), reprinted by permission of Bloodaxe Books.

Greta Thunberg: transcript of speech by Greta Thunberg at UN Climate Change Conference in Katowice, Poland, December 2018 reprinted by permission of Penguin Random House Ltd.

Louisa Waugh: extract from 'Letters from Tsengal', Mongolia 1998 in *Letters from the Edge: 12 Women of the World Write Home* edited by Chris Brazier (New Internationalist, 2008), reprinted by permission of the publishers.

Damon Weaver: Damon Weaver: interview with President Barack Obama on election night from abcnews.go.com/GMA/ reprinted by permission of Mrs Regina Weaver, mother of late Damon Weaver.

H.G. Wells: extract from *The Time Machine* (Penguin, 2007), reprinted by permission of Penguin Random House Inc.

Vivienne Westwood: extract from *Vivienne Westwood, Get a Life: The Diaries of Vivienne Westwood 2010–2016* (Serpent's Tail, 2016), reprinted with permission of publisher.

William Carlos Williams: 'Landscape with the Fall of Icarus' from *The Collected Poems: Volume II*, 1939-1962 (Carcanet, 2000), copyright © William Carlos Williams 1962, reprinted by permission of the publishers, New Directions Publishing Corp. and Carcanet Press Ltd.

Émile Zola: extract from *The Ladies' Paradise*, first published 1883 translated by Brian Nelson, © Oxford University Press July 2008, reprinted with permission of publisher via PLS Clear.

ASME: extract from '5 Young Inventors Aim to Change the World' © 2022 The American Society of Mechanical Engineers. Reprinted with permission of ASME.

Textile Value Chain: 'Oxfordshire Teenager Launches Sustainable Fashion Line' © Textile Value Chain, reprinted with permission of Textile Value Chain.

Rachel Redford: retelling of 'Daedalus and Icarus'; written for the first edition and reused by permission of the author.

Any third-party use of this material, outside this publication, is prohibited. Interested parties should apply to the copyright holders indicated in each case.

Every effort has been made to contact copyright holders of material reproduced in this book. Any omissions will be rectified in subsequent printings if notice is given to the publisher.

Contents

How important is friendship to us?

> 'Make new friends but keep the old. One is silver and the other gold.'
>
> European proverb

Talk about ...

- How do we value different types of friendship?
- Do we function better with others by our side?
- What do our friends reveal about us?
- What are some of the challenges of making and keeping friends?

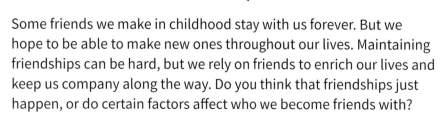

Language tip

-*ship* is a noun suffix. When added to an already existing noun, it puts emphasis on the more general status or condition. As well as 'friendship', other examples include 'companionship', 'membership', 'partnership', 'relationship'.

Some friends we make in childhood stay with us forever. But we hope to be able to make new ones throughout our lives. Maintaining friendships can be hard, but we rely on friends to enrich our lives and keep us company along the way. Do you think that friendships just happen, or do certain factors affect who we become friends with?

Think about the many different types and expressions of friendship as you work through the texts in this unit.

An expert's view
Read what a psychologist says about friendship in a magazine article.

- Examine how a writer's use of language and grammatical features creates effect and meaning
- Discuss the meaning and effect of new and unfamiliar words

Q&A: Friendship

Why do we make the friends we do?
Friends are people who regularly cross our paths, for example our classmates or our team-mates. But why do we become friends with one particular classmate rather than another? Perhaps we both like the same football team or perhaps we are both computer
5 geeks – whatever it is, we have things in common.

How does acquaintanceship develop into friendship?
The key is self-disclosure. "Can I talk to you for a minute?" or "May I share something with you?" are questions which could move an acquaintanceship into a friendship. You are taking the risk of disclosing information about yourself, but the acquaintanceship is not going to
10 develop unless there is reciprocity. If your acquaintance listens to what you have to say – perhaps about your problems at school – but does not tell you anything personal in return, there is no reciprocity. That acquaintanceship is not going to become a friendship.

Why do some friends stick while others don't?
Having established a friendship through self-disclosure and
15 reciprocity, the glue that binds it is intimacy. This involves emotional expression and support, followed by acceptance, loyalty and trust. Our friends are always there for us through thick and thin – but there are limits. If a friend is overcritical of our clothes or our behaviour, the friendship may not last. On the other hand, if our friend asks for
20 help, we will value the friendship more highly.

Learning tip
This text is made up of many **complex compound sentences**. Pay close attention to the use of prepositions, conjunctions and conditional phrases.

Language tip
Conditional sentences express truths or possibilities where one thing can cause another to happen. They are usually composed of at least two clauses joined by a co-ordinating conjunction, such as 'if', 'unless', 'since' or 'but'.

The conditional can also be expressed using comparative clauses, such as 'The more … the better … '.

Glossary

psychologist expert in the study of the mind

self-disclosure revealing a fact or information about yourself

acquaintance person you know slightly, not a close friend

reciprocity doing the same by return

intimacy the condition of being close, as in a relationship

facilitate make easier

- Examine how a writer's use of language and grammatical features creates effect and meaning
- Discuss ideas with others, questioning and evaluating opposing views

How do we stay friends?

Four basic behaviours have been identified by psychologists as necessary to maintain a friendship:

1. self-disclosure
2. supportiveness
3. interaction
4. keeping the friendship positive

25 These first two (self-disclosure and supportiveness) are facilitated by communication. We must be willing to share our lives, listen, and offer support. Sometimes we might be worried or upset by something in our subconscious mind, and talking openly to a friend can help us to work out what it is and how we can make it better. The third (interaction)
30 involves spending time together, while the fourth (keeping the friendship positive) means considering the quality of the relationship. Self-disclosure doesn't just mean offloading or letting off steam. The intimacy which makes a friendship thrive must be enjoyable and nurturing for both of you. The more rewarding a friendship, the better we feel about it
35 and the more willing we are to make an effort to keep it alive.

Comprehension

1 What is the article about?
2 What does 'Q&A' stand for?
3 Who is this article aimed at?

1 Find as many examples as you can of nouns using the suffix *-ship*.
2 Find examples of conditional sentences in the text.
3 Explain the meaning of the following idioms:
   a 'cross our paths' (line 1)
   b 'through thick and thin' (line 17)
   c 'on the other hand' (line 19)
4 How is the article structured to make the information clear and easy to understand?

1 Do you agree with what the psychologist says? Explain your answer.
2 Discuss and compare examples of friendships, either your own or those you know about from books, TV shows or films.
3 Do you have a favourite fictional representation of friendship?

Language tip
Idiomatic language is often difficult to understand or translate. Idioms are words and phrases that mean something more than just their literal meaning. Popular idiomatic expressions about friendship in English include 'Like two peas in a pod' or 'To be as thick as thieves'.

Talk about ...
- What other idiomatic expressions can you think of that capture the power and the problems of friendship?
- When do you know you are on shaky ground with a friendship?

Filling in the friendship wall

Make sure you understand the vocabulary in the article you have just read by filling in the gaps in the 'friendship wall' below. Write the words down in your notebook or on a separate piece of paper. All the words appear in the text 'Q&A: Friendship'.

- Understand the meaning and effect of new and unfamiliar words
- Write non-fiction texts
- Make sure text type, structure and style are suitable for the audience

Communication is needed to [f_____] two basic behaviours necessary for binding a friendship. (10 letters)

If you tell an acquaintance about an emotional difficulty you are experiencing and he or she does not [r_____], then you are not going to become real friends. (11 letters)

What really makes friends stick together is [i_____]. (8 letters)

Within a friendship, friends need to express their [e_____]. (8 letters)

A friendship needs to be positive and [n_____] for both of you. (9 letters)

If you are not willing to [d_____] personal details about yourself, you will not develop an acquaintanceship into a friendship. (8 letters)

To be a loyal friend, you need to be [s_____] and be willing to [h_____] your friend if you possibly can. (10 and 4 letters)

You need to maintain the bond of friendship through [i_____], otherwise the friendship will not last. (11 letters)

Not everyone agrees with what [p_____] say. Do you? (13 letters)

Stretch zone

Write some sentences that include all ten words you added to the friendship wall.

Join a friendship club!

Write an advertisement for a new friendship club for your school magazine or newsletter.

- Make the requirements for membership of the group as open and inclusive as possible.
- Think of ways to make your new club sound exciting and emphasize that it is an opportunity to connect people who may be compatible and have interests in common.

- Use texts as a model for own writing
- Examine and discuss a wide range of texts
- Proofread and edit writing
- Participate fully in discussions

Ancient Greek philosophy

There have been many different theories of friendship. The following extract is by the ancient Greek philosopher Aristotle who lived from 384 BCE to 322 BCE (more than 2,300 years ago). He stated that there are three types of friendship, but only one true, or 'perfect', type.

The three kinds of friendship

Friendship based on utility. Utility ... changes according to circumstances. Friendships of this kind seem to occur most frequently among those who are pursuing their own advantage. Such persons do not spend much time together, because sometimes
5   they do not even like one another, and therefore feel no need of such an association unless they are mutually useful. So with the disappearance of the grounds for friendship, the friendship also breaks up, because that was what kept it alive.

Friendship based on pleasure. Friendship between young people
10   is thought to be grounded on pleasure, because their chief interest is in their own pleasure and the opportunity of the moment. As the years go by, however, their tastes change too, so that they are quick to make and to break friendships; because their affection changes just as the things that please them do.
15   That is why they fall in and out of friendship quickly, changing their attitude often within the same day.

Perfect friendship is based on goodness. Only the friendship of those who are good, and similar in their goodness, is perfect. For these people each alike wish good for the other, and they
20   are good in themselves. And it is those who desire the good of their friends for the friends' sake that are most truly friends, because each loves the other for what he is, and not for any incidental quality. Friendship of this kind is permanent, because in it are united all the attributes that friends ought to have.

From *The Nicomachean Ethics* by ARISTOTLE

Talk about ...

Are there any other types of friendship that Aristotle doesn't talk about?

Language tip
Writing with conviction
means a writer presents their view or argument with an absolute belief in it.

Aristotle presents his views on friendship with conviction. He doesn't say 'I think' or 'Perhaps'. He presents all of his ideas as statements of fact. For example, he asserts, 'There are three kinds of friendship.' This is arguably not a fact, but Aristotle is demonstrating his absolute belief that it is true.

Writing with conviction

Write a statement presenting your ideas on the value of friendship.

- Explain what you think are the most important qualities in a friend and why those qualities are important.
- Now read your statement to a partner. Is your partner convinced by what you say? Listen to their writing and give feedback.

True friendship: a flowing river?

How do friendships change over time?

In the following poem, the British poet Brian Jones remembers a perfect childhood friendship, and how he felt when he met his friend again after twenty years.

- Examine how a writer's use of language and grammatical features creates effect and meaning
- Consider how poets play with themes and conventions in a range of poetic forms
- Investigate the origin of words

About Friends

The good thing about friends
is not having to finish sentences.

I sat a whole summer afternoon with my friend once
on a river bank, bashing heels on the baked mud
5   and watching the small chunks slide into the water
and listening to them – plop plop plop.
He said, 'I like the twigs when they ... you know ...
like that.' I said, 'There's that branch ...'
We both said, 'Mmmm.' The river flowed and flowed
10 and there were lots of butterflies, that afternoon.

I first thought there was a sad thing about friends
when we met twenty years later.
We both talked hundreds of sentences,
taking care to finish all we said,
15 and explain it all very carefully,
as if we'd been discovered in places
we should not be, and were somehow ashamed.

I understood then what the river meant by flowing.

BRIAN JONES

Word origins

friend (n), from the Old English word *frēond*, coming from the verb meaning 'love' (in Old English, *frēo(ga)n*)
Related words:
- befriend   • friendship

Comprehension

1 What was so special about the writer's childhood friendship?

2 How had the way they communicated as children changed when the two friends met again twenty years later?

1 How does the poem use language in a structured way that makes it different to a novel or short story?

1 In the first part of the poem, the river 'flowed and flowed'. How do you imagine this scene?

2 In the last line of the poem the flowing of the river has a metaphorical meaning. What is it?

Requirements for a best friend?

In this poem, another British poet, Elizabeth Jennings, is perhaps unusually honest about what she is looking for in a friend.

Friends

I fear it's very wrong of me,
And yet I must admit,
When someone offers friendship
I want the *whole* of it.
5 I don't want everybody else
To share my friends with me.
At least, I want one special one,
Who, indisputably

Likes me much more than all the rest,
10 Who's always on my side,
Who never cares what others say.
Who lets me come and hide
Within his shadow, in his house –
It doesn't matter where –
15 Who lets me simply be myself,
Who's always, *always* there.

ELIZABETH JENNINGS

- Consider how poets play with themes and conventions in a range of poetic forms
- Compare and contrast a wide range of texts in the same theme
- Discuss ideas with others, questioning and evaluating opposing views

Language tip
Anaphora is an effective poetic device where the same word or phrase is used at the start of a sentence or line of poetry for emphasis. For example, the repetition of 'Who' in the poem 'Friends'.

Comprehension

1 List all the ways in which 'About Friends' (on the previous page) and 'Friends' are different in their uses of poetic devices.
2 List all the ways in which 'About Friends' and 'Friends' are similar in their uses of poetic devices.

1 In 'Friends', what does the poet want from her friend? Do you think it is 'very wrong' of her to want what she does?
2 How would you describe this type of friendship?
3 What emotional qualities does she have which would make her the sort of friend you would or would not like?
4 Which line or lines in the poem do you most agree with? Quote the words and explain why you have chosen them.

Learning tip
When you are comparing two poems, be sure to consider similarities and differences in rhythm, rhyme, line length, repetition, narrative voice, dialogue and choice of words.

Now you're the poet!

Write your own poem about friendship. Make it real by writing with conviction and honesty, perhaps focusing on a specific example from your own life. What do you think makes a good friend? Are some friendships deeper and more lasting than others?

- Consider point of view. It could be written in the first person ('I'), in the second person ('You'), or in the third person ('he', 'she', 'they').
- Make a note of the poetic devices you use.
- Read out your poem to your partner or group. Start a conversation afterwards by giving some background to what inspired you.

- Use literary and rhetorical devices to enhance the impact of writing
- Write a range of fiction genres and poetry
- Understand and write from different points of view

Talk about ...

The poet Elizabeth Jennings presents a very different sense of personal conviction to Aristotle. As a woman who lived in the twentieth century, she writes of her fears and doubts and what it means to be a sensitive person.

- Is this a more convincing and sympathetic position to read about today?
- How do the more personal reflections of poets like Elizabeth Jennings and Brian Jones compare to theories of friendship, like that of Aristotle?

Online friends

Online friends can be a great way to explore new interests, or get to know people from other parts of the world. Read the following requests for online friends from 14-year-old students in different parts of the world.

- Examine closely how texts mirror the time and place in which they are written
- Examine how a writer's use of language and grammatical features creates effect and meaning

✉ New message — ↗ ✕

Hi, I'm Rob from Florida, USA, where there's lots of sunshine. What I'm really into is computer games and computers generally. I had my first computer from my mom when I was five and I've been a geek ever since! I've been designing interactive games over the last couple of years and that's what I really want to do big time when I graduate. I'm looking for an online friend who shares my enthusiasm – or is just as kooky as me! I want to create new games with new ideas from someone from another culture so we can create together. Japan or China would be really cool.

✉ New message — ↗ ✕

Hi, I'm Rosetta from Singapore. I'm the youngest in a family of five girls. My eldest sister has graduated now and works in an insurance company in the city. My real love in life is fashion and clothes. I'm WILD about them. What I do is study the clothes in magazines and on television and I get ideas and design my own things. We have great fabric markets here – Chinese silks and all sorts – so I can afford to look like a beauty queen! I'd like an online friend who loves fashion and lives somewhere where there are different kinds of fabrics. I'd love to swap ideas and designs. That's what I really want to do with my life – be a designer.

✉ New message — ↗ ✕

Hi, I'm Jessie from Sweden. I live in a small town on the coast of Sweden. We have been learning English since we were very small at school, so we speak English very well. (I don't want to sound boastful, but we do!) Sometimes I think it's really boring here and I'd love to have an online friend from far away, like in Africa or China. I want to know what everyday life is like for you. What is your school like? Do you have lots of rules? What do you learn about? What books do you read? Tell me, tell me! I can help you with your English.

Talk about ...

- What do you think are the advantages of having an online, or 'virtual', friend?
- Some people say that chatting to 'virtual' friends on blogs or in online chat rooms is not a proper substitute for real life. It could even be dangerous. Do you agree?

Glossary

kooky (*informal*) slightly strange and unusual, but in a likeable way

- Use punctuation to reflect thoughts, feelings and how words are spoken
- Use informal vocabulary to create effect in writing
- Adapt writing style and register for intended audience and purpose

> ✉ New message ─ ↗ ✕
>
> Hi, I'm Jake from Australia. Just like in all the movies and soap operas you've ever seen about Australia, we spend a lot of our lives on the beach surfing and having barbecues. But I tell you what really interests me and that's FOOD! I love it. I just love Thai food with all those limes and ginger, and I'd like an online friend in Thailand. Do you eat just traditional Thai food at home, or do you have fast food like chips and burgers? What do you like best? Do you and your family eat together every day at home? Do you eat outside like us on the beach?

> ✉ New message ─ ↗ ✕
>
> Hi, I'm Irina from Russia. I live with my mother and four brothers in a town in the east of Russia. Life is not easy here because there used to be a factory here which employed two thousand people, but now it has closed and there is no work. Winter is very long and very cold. Snow is 5 metres high and stays for months. I study hard so that I can learn perfect English and go to Moscow to study when I'm older. I would like an online friend who I can practise my English with. I would like to talk about your school and the job opportunities in your country. What is your family life like? What do you do in your spare time? I watch movies at home and help my mother with the shopping and housework.

Writing to an online friend

- Choose one of these online friends to reply to. Explain who you are and where you live, and tell them a little about your interests and daily life. Ask questions of your own so that your online friend will have plenty to respond to.
- Then write your own request for an online friend, using the texts on these pages as models. Include information about yourself, and what you would like from your online friend.

Use informal language appropriate to your peer group and to suit the online environment and chat space, and make effective use of punctuation.

Stretch zone

Script a conversation between two people making friends in an online chat room. It could be related to a particular interest (like a shared love of sport, cookery or a TV series).

When friends grow apart

This story is set in a mining town in Australia called Yirrkala. The mining industry has had an enormous impact on the local Aboriginal community, who have inhabited the area for over 40,000 years. The novel was written by Clare Atkins, a teacher and script writer, who lived among the Aboriginal people in Arnhem Land while writing the book. The story follows the difficulties of growing up, as well as the clash of two cultures in Australia today.

In this extract, Rosie, the narrator and a white girl, is surprised to see her childhood best friend Nona, from the Aboriginal community, return to school. Nona has been away for many years and, in her absence, Rosie has become friendly with some popular, and wealthy, white girls who do not understand the Aboriginal people and their way of life.

- Examine and discuss a wide range of texts
- Identify evidence in a text about the environment, culture and social situation

A friend from the past

Nona reaches out and takes the comprehension sheet.

Miss Fuller smiles nervously. "Okay, great."

She gives Nona a pen and paper.

Nona's voice used to be full of laughter, like even her insides
5 were grinning. But now it comes out soft and flat. "You got a pencil?"

"Sorry?"

"Pencil."

"Oh. Yes. Sure."

10 Miss Fuller gets her one. Selena smirks. She writes on the side of her exercise book, nudging it over so I can read.

What are we – in primary school?

I force a smile. I tell myself the words are harmless, just a joke.

I watch Nona as she starts to work. She begins by colouring
15 in the holes in the letters – the a's, the o's, the d's, the e's. By the end of the lesson they are all filled in. I lean forward and see she's also drawn in the left margin, decorating it with swirls and … are they turtles? I can't quite make out from my desk. It's beautiful, though. Shades of grey-lead ocean.

20 Selena catches me looking and underlines her previous words:

primary school

Miss Fuller passes Nona and sees what she's doing. I wait for a reaction but our teacher just nods and smiles and walks on.

Language tip
Superlative adjectives are useful for dramatic emphasis or comparison. They are formed by adding the suffix *-est* to the adjective, as in 'big<u>gest</u>', 'loud<u>est</u>', 'smal<u>lest</u>'. Some longer adjectives, however, cannot be made into superlatives by adding the suffix. Instead, the superlative is formed as an adjective phrase using the words 'most' and 'least'. For example: 'My friend is the <u>kindest</u>, <u>funniest</u>, <u>most sensible</u>, <u>least selfish</u> person you will ever meet.'

Glossary

detention form of punishment where a student has to stay behind after school has finished
old man (*informal*) father
P's (*Australian, informal*) driving licence

- Examine and discuss a wide range of texts
- Identify evidence in a text about the environment, culture and social situation

Selena whispers, "Can you imagine if one of *us* did that?"

25 Selena always talks like that. Us and them. Ŋäpaki and Yolŋu.

She's right, though. If a Ŋäpaki kid – a non-Aboriginal kid – did that Miss Fuller would be telling them to start working or stay and do it in detention.

Selena articulates the question this time. "You know her?"

30 I want to say yes. I want to say, *She's my sister. She was my best friend.* But I know Selena would find that crazy and I don't want to explain. So I say, "She knows my mum."

"From the art centre?"

I nod, convincing myself it's easier this way.

35 The bell goes and we throw our timelines onto Miss Fuller's desk as we stream out to our next classes. Selena moves off. She chose Cert One in Business as an elective, which is ridiculous. She hates anything to do with maths, and thinks the only function of the economy is to determine how much stuff from
40 the US costs online. But her old man said she should do it, so she did. And Anya chose it because Selena did. I couldn't bring myself to study something I'd never use. I figured Hospitality at least might help me get a job in town once I get my P's.

I feel someone touch my arm. I look down and see a dark-
45 brown hand. Long fingernails. A pale palm.

I hear her voice say, "*Yapa.*" Sister. And suddenly I'm six years old again. We're in my bedroom holding hands.

I look up at Nona. "Mum said you were back."

"Got here last week."

50 "Are you living at your grandma's?"

Nona shakes her head. "In Birritjimi. My aunty's house. You remember Tina? She just had a baby, a little boy. We're living with them – me, my mum and the
55 smalls."

I smile at the mention of her two little sisters; they're only a couple of years younger than us, but we always called them the smalls to make ourselves feel bigger. Nona smiles shyly back at me.
60 There is so much to say. So much I want to know. But I can feel Selena and Anya watching us. They're standing outside

> **Language tip**
> Writers have many tools they can use to **create emphasis**. These include using typographic features like **italics** and **exclamation marks!** A more literary technique is known as amplification.
>
> **Amplification** repeats a word or expression for emphasis, often using additional adjectives to clarify the meaning. For example, 'Love, real love, takes time' is an example of amplification.
>
> Find examples of amplification on this page.

- Use literary and rhetorical devices to enhance the impact of writing
- Use other texts as a model for own writing
- Perform roleplay, speaking fluently and with confidence

their classroom, waiting to go in. Selena makes eye contact and frowns, as if to say, *What are you doing?* I remember what school was like before she came. Me and Anya, always on the periphery. Not a real group, just two loners clinging desperately together. It was years ago but it was yesterday. I feel sick.

70 I turn back to Nona. My words come out abruptly. "I'd better go. See you round."

I see Nona's face fall, a crumple of confusion. And then I'm walking away.

From *Nona and Me* by CLARE ATKINS

Comprehension

 A

1 What do we learn about Selena's character from the extract? Give evidence from the extract to support your answer.
2 What opinion do you have of Nona's personality?

 B

1 Explain what 'a crumple of confusion' means at the end of the extract. (line 72)
2 Explain how the use of repetition and amplification reinforce Rosie's ethical dilemma.
3 What are the disadvantages of reading the story from Rosie's point of view?

 C

1 What short phrase tells the reader that Selena is prejudiced against those from a different background to hers?
2 What are the two moments when Rosie shows she is ashamed of knowing Nona? Explain why Rosie rejects Nona at the end of the extract. How did this make Nona feel?
3 How do you know that Rosie has, in fact, different attitudes and beliefs to Selena and Anya? Give evidence from the text.

A tricky conversation!

Think of a reason why you might have to stop seeing so much of a friend who has been important to you. Perhaps you are moving to another part of town, or another city? Perhaps your friend has changed in a way you cannot relate to? Your friend may be very understanding, or perhaps they will get angry and you will need to try to pacify them.

- Write down the dialogue for your difficult conversation as a script or through reported speech.
- Use rhetorical devices for emphasis, emotional tension and impact.
- Work with a partner to perform the dialogue, like a play reading.
- Ask for feedback to further develop your script.

Glossary

pacify to calm a person down

Making a new friend

In the following extract, Lucy has been evacuated from London to escape the bombing during the Second World War and she is staying in the large, old house of Professor Kirke. While exploring, she walks through a wardrobe and finds herself in the land of Narnia. She is in a forest full of snow, and stands for a while under the lamp-post, before she sees Mr Tumnus, the faun. A faun is a mythological creature resembling a goat or a type of deer, with cloven hooves. In this extract, they strike up an unlikely friendship.

- Examine and discuss a wide range of texts
- Identify evidence in a text about the environment, culture and social situation

Meeting Mr Tumnus

"Good Evening," said Lucy. But the Faun was so busy picking up its parcels that at first it did not reply. When it had finished it made her a little bow.

"Good evening, good evening," said the Faun. "Excuse me
5 – I don't want to be inquisitive – but should I be right in thinking that you are a Daughter of Eve?"

"My name's Lucy," said she, not quite understanding him.

"But you are – forgive me – you are what they call a girl?" asked the Faun.

10 "Of course I'm a girl," said Lucy.

"You are in fact Human?"

"Of course I'm human," said Lucy, still a little puzzled.

"To be sure, to be sure," said the Faun. "How stupid of me! But I've never seen a Son of Adam or a Daughter of
15 Eve before. I am delighted, delighted," it went on. "Allow me to introduce myself. My name is Tumnus."

"I am very pleased to meet you, Mr Tumnus," said Lucy.

"And may I ask, O Lucy Daughter of Eve," said Mr Tumnus, "how you have come into Narnia?"

20 "Narnia? What's that?" said Lucy.

Talk about ...
- What do you think of the writer's ability to make a mythological or imaginary creature come across as someone we can relate to?
- Is this unlikely friendship a useful metaphor for making other kinds of friendships?

- Examine and discuss a wide range of texts
- Identify evidence in a text about the environment, culture and social situation
- Read literature from different historical periods

"This is the land of Narnia," said the Faun, "where we are now; all that lies between the lamp-post and the great castle of Cair Paravel on the eastern sea. And you – you have come from the wild woods of the west?"

25 "I – I got in through the wardrobe in the spare room," said Lucy.

"Ah!" said Mr Tumnus in a rather melancholy voice, "if only I had worked harder at geography when I was a little Faun, I should no doubt know all about those strange countries. It is too late now."

30 "But they aren't countries at all," said Lucy, almost laughing. "It's only just back there – at least – I'm not sure. It is summer there."

"Meanwhile," said Mr Tumnus, "it is winter in Narnia, and has been for ever so long, and we shall both catch cold if we
35 stand here talking in the snow. Daughter of Eve from the far land of Spare Oom where eternal summer reigns around the bright city of War Drobe, how would it be if you came and had tea with me?"

"Thank you very much, Mr Tumnus," said Lucy. "But I
40 ought to be getting back."

"It's only just round the corner," said the Faun, "and there'll be a roaring fire – and toast – and sardines – and cake."

"Well, it's very kind of you," said Lucy. "But I shan't be able to stay long."

45 "If you will take my arm, Daughter of Eve," said Mr Tumnus, "I shall be be able to hold the umbrella over both of us. That's the way. Now – off we go."

And so Lucy found herself walking through the wood arm in arm with this strange creature as if they had known one
50 another all their lives.

They had not gone far before they came to a rocky place with little hills up and little hills down. At the bottom of one small valley Mr Tumnus turned suddenly aside as if he were going to walk straight into an unusually large rock, but at
55 the last moment Lucy found he was leading her into the entrance of a cave. As soon as they were inside she found

Glossary

inquisitive always asking questions or trying to find out things
melancholy sad or gloomy
geography study of the Earth's surface and its physical features, climate, products and population

Language tip
Some tips for writing realistic dialogue and narrative text:

- Don't overdo the speech tags (such as 'said Lucy'), just use them when it is necessary to distinguish who is speaking.
- Include exclamations and speech effects, such as the occasional stumble with words.
- Sometimes use more informal language structures, like starting a sentence with 'And' or 'But'.

Do you think it's possible to become good friends with someone quickly, as Lucy and Mr Tumnus do? Are some friendships 'more genuine' than others?

- Explain how an author develops character, setting and plot
- Look at how texts are structured and presented in order to influence the reader's point of view

herself blinking in the light of a wood fire. "Now we shan't be long," he said, and immediately put a kettle on.

Lucy thought she had never been in a nicer place. It was a little, dry, clean cave of reddish stone with a carpet on the floor and two little chairs ("one for me and one for a friend," said Mr Tumnus) and a table and dresser and a mantelpiece over the fire and above that a picture of an old Faun with a grey beard. In one corner there was a door which Lucy thought must lead to Mr Tumnus's bedroom, and on one wall was a shelf full of books. Lucy looked at these while he was setting out the tea things. [...]

"Now, Daughter of Eve!" said the Faun.

And really it was a wonderful tea. There was a nice brown egg, lightly boiled, for each of them, and then sardines on toast, and then buttered toast, and then toast with honey, and then a sugar-topped cake. And when Lucy was tired of eating, the Faun began to talk. He had wonderful tales to tell of life in the forest. He told about the midnight dances and how the Nymphs who lived in the wells and the Dryads who lived in the trees came out to dance with the Fauns; about long hunting parties after the milk-white stag who could give you wishes if you caught him; about feasting and treasure-seeking with the wild Red Dwarfs in deep mines and caverns far beneath the forest floor; and then about summer when the woods were green and old Silenus on his fat donkey would come to visit them, and sometimes Bacchus himself, and the whole forest would give itself up to its jollification for weeks on end.

From *The Lion, the Witch and the Wardrobe* by C.S. Lewis

Comprehension

1 Other than 'Human', how does Mr Tumnus refer to Lucy?
2 What does Lucy like about Mr Tumnus?
3 What does she find so reassuring about his manners and behaviour?
4 What is so comforting about his home?

1 Geography is a discipline (an area of study) of its own, but geographical location and a sense of place can be very important in literature. How important is geography to understanding the conversation between Lucy and Mr Tumnus?

Stretch zone

Write your own story of a friendly encounter with a creature of another species.

Mapping Narnia

Draw a map of the imaginary world that frames the encounter between Lucy and Mr Tumnus.

- Include all the built features, as well as the natural geography, and write in the place names (such as Spare Oom, Place of Eternal Summer).
- Chart the journey of the two different characters on your map and include a key (also known as a legend) to explain the symbols you use.
- Add a title to your map.

A chat with the actors

The following extract is from an interview with the actors Georgie Henley and James McAvoy, who starred in the film version of the novel, *The Chronicles of Narnia: The Lion, the Witch and the Wardrobe*. They discuss the friendship that grew between them in real life, as it did in the story. When they started filming, Georgie was only ten years old. This was her first acting role.

- Look at how texts are structured and presented to influence the reader's point of view
- Identify evidence in a text about the environment, culture and social situation

Georgie Henley and James McAvoy

Q: Why does Lucy follow Mr Tumnus home?

GEORGIE: She does it because she really trusts in Mr Tumnus. They're almost like long-lost friends, and there's no point in having long-lost friends if you don't
5 go into tea with them.

JAMES: The thing that is so special about them is they're nearly the same person in a lot of ways, even though he's 150 and she's eight years old. When they meet each other it is fast friends immediately ...

10 **GEORGIE:** They connect.

Q: How did shooting in chronological order help you?

GEORGIE: We got more mature, really. In the earliest shoots I was a bit of a spitfire on set, I was really hyper
15 on set, wasn't I?

JAMES: You were a bit hyper on set. But I didn't help, I was jumping around like I was seven.

GEORGIE: You were? It did help me.

JAMES: I think so. You guys got more experienced, more
20 chilled out. And you got so much more comfortable by the end.

GEORGIE: And you became more faun-ey. More goat-like.

JAMES: My beard got longer. [...] That was my favourite thing, watching you grow. You all grew inches
25 during this film.

Talk about ...

- What makes a good opening question in an interview?
- Consider the many different types of interviews you have read or listened to and how they are scripted.
- What works and what doesn't work, in your opinion?

Glossary

spitfire something or someone who behaves in an angry or explosive manner

hyper from the Greek word for 'over' or 'beyond', is often used as a short form of **hyperactive**, which means excessively active; unable to be still or concentrate

to chill or be **chilled out** is to relax and enjoy yourself

Q: **Did you keep track on the wall?**

GEORGIE: Yeah. Skandar (Keynes) grew six and a half inches, I did four inches, William (Moseley) grew two inches, and Anna (Popplewell) grew half an inch.

30

Q: **How did they keep up with your costumes?**

GEORGIE: They just … had to keep doing them again and again and again. It was so weird, do you remember when Will stood up and his fur coat ripped in the back? So wardrobe was, like, seriously stressing, because these were real fur coats.

35

Q: **James, did you want Mr Tumnus to wear a shirt for the coronation?**

JAMES: No, he's too scruffy for that, my friend.

40 GEORGIE: Scruffy!

JAMES: Well, you know, it's the faun's way, isn't it? Classically speaking, fauns are followers of Dionysus and Bacchus and they make reference to that in the book. They were free, they were unrestricted … It was all about being open. That's why, I think, it was a good choice to make Tumnus a faun, because he's about openness, which is what he and Lucy have in common.

45

Q: **What was the hardest thing about filming the movie?**

50

GEORGIE: Being away from my friends and family.

JAMES: Yeah, being away from my loved ones for so long. You know, New Zealand is twenty-four hours from London. I couldn't go home for a few days, it was difficult. It's hard to call. Emails are the best way.

55

GEORGIE: Emails and phone calls. And letters. I wrote letters to school.

- Look at how texts are structured and presented in order to influence the reader's point of view
- Identify evidence in a text about the environment, culture and social situation
- Identify the grammar and vocabulary of formal and informal registers

Comprehension

A

1 Why was this role a particular challenge for Georgie?

2 The connection between the characters on-screen and off-screen is a major focus of this interview. Summarize the information that demonstrates this special relationship.

B

1 Find examples of informal vocabulary and language structures used in the interview. Look back at the Language tip on page 18 to help you. What effect do they have on the reader and on how we view the speakers?

C

1 What are the challenges of writing and acting non-human characters?

2 Discuss how you would go about finding an appropriate location to film a work of fantasy fiction like Narnia.

2 Travel

What is it like to go on a journey?

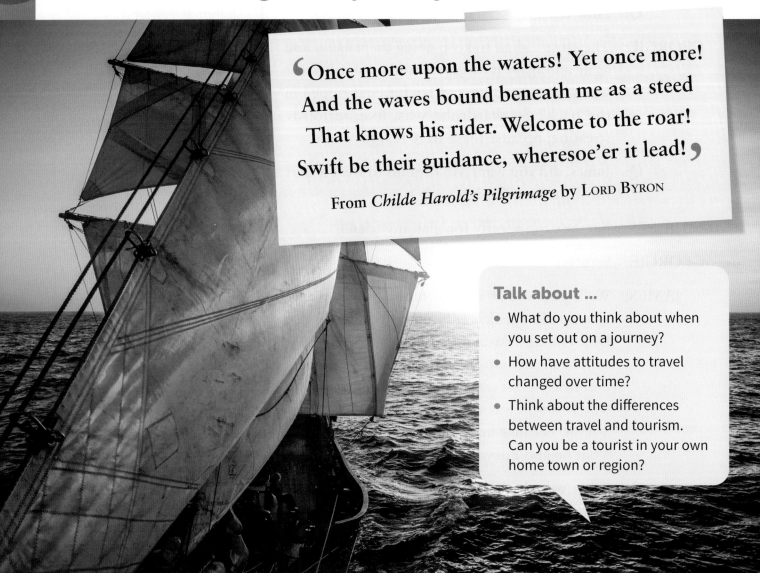

'Once more upon the waters! Yet once more!
And the waves bound beneath me as a steed
That knows his rider. Welcome to the roar!
Swift be their guidance, wheresoe'er it lead!'

From *Childe Harold's Pilgrimage* by LORD BYRON

Talk about ...

- What do you think about when you set out on a journey?
- How have attitudes to travel changed over time?
- Think about the differences between travel and tourism. Can you be a tourist in your own home town or region?

In the early nineteenth century, when British poet Lord Byron wrote the poem quoted above, few people had the opportunity to travel far. For those who did get to explore distant lands, the journey could be long and hazardous.

By the time French author Jules Verne wrote his novel *Around the World in Eighty Days* (published in 1872), the opportunities for travel had opened up considerably. As he wrote, 'The world has grown smaller, since a man can now round it ten times more quickly than a hundred years ago.'

A fictional journey

In the following extract from *Around the World in Eighty Days,* Phileas Fogg, a wealthy English gentleman, has returned home early from his London club. He has just accepted a challenge from his fellow club members to travel around the world in eighty days.

Jean Passepartout, his French servant, will be his travelling companion. This is Passepartout's first day of employment and he is shocked at the sudden turn of events.

- Consider the influence of literature from different historical periods
- Investigate the origin of words

Caricature of Jules Verne

In which Phileas Fogg Astounds Passepartout, his Servant

Phileas Fogg, at twenty-five minutes past seven, left the Reform Club.

Passepartout, who had studied the programme of his duties, was more than surprised to see his master guilty of the inexactness
5 of appearing at this unaccustomed hour; for, according to the rule, he was not due in Saville Row until precisely midnight.

Mr. Fogg went to his bedroom, and called out, "Passepartout!"

Passepartout did not reply. It was not the right hour.

"Passepartout!" repeated Mr. Fogg, without raising his voice.

10 Passepartout made his appearance.

"I've called you twice," observed his master.

"But it is not midnight," responded the other, showing his watch.

"I know it; I don't blame you. We start for Dover and Calais in ten minutes."

15 A puzzled grin spread over Passepartout's round face; clearly he had not understood his master.

"Monsieur is going to leave home?"

"Yes," returned Phileas Fogg. "We are going round the world."

Passepartout opened his eyes wide, raised his eyebrows, held
20 up his hands, and seemed about to collapse, so overcome was he with astonishment.

"Round the world!" he murmured.

Word origins

journey (n), comes from the French word *journée,* meaning 'work' or 'distance completed in a day'
Related words:
- journal
- journalist

Glossary

caricature amusing or exaggerated picture or description of a person
Passepartout name of Phileas Fogg's servant, from the French *passe-partout,* from *passer* ('to pass') and *partout* ('everywhere')

"In eighty days," responded Mr. Fogg. "So we haven't a moment to lose."

25 "But the trunks?" gasped Passepartout, unconsciously swaying his head from right to left.

"We'll have no trunks; only a carpet-bag, with two shirts and three pairs of stockings for me, and the same for you. We'll buy our clothes on the way. Bring down my mackintosh and
30 travelling-cloak, and some stout shoes, though we shall do little walking. Make haste!"

Passepartout tried to reply, but could not. He went up to his own room, fell into a chair, and muttered: "That's good, that is! And all I wanted was a quiet life!"

35 He mechanically set about making the preparations for departure. Around the world in eighty days! Was his master a fool? No. Was this a joke, then? They were going to Dover; good! To Calais; good again! After all, Passepartout, who had been away from France five years, would not be sorry to set foot on his
40 native soil again. Perhaps they would go as far as Paris, and it would do his eyes good to see Paris once more. But surely a gentleman unwilling to take so many steps would stop there … this person who had previously had such an orderly domestic life!

By eight o'clock Passepartout had packed the modest carpet-
45 bag, then, still troubled in mind, he carefully shut the door of his room, and descended the stairs to Mr. Fogg.

Mr. Fogg was quite ready. Under his arm might have been observed a red-bound copy of Bradshaw's Continental Railway Steam Transit and General Guide, with its timetables showing
50 the arrival and departure of steamboats and railways. He took the carpet-bag, opened it, and slipped into it a goodly roll of Bank of England notes, which would pass wherever he might go.

"You have forgotten nothing?" asked he.

"Nothing, monsieur."

55 "My mackintosh and cloak?"

"Here they are."

- Examine how a writer's use of language and grammatical features creates effect and meaning
- Consider the influence of literature from different historical periods

Glossary

trunk chest or box used to store things in
mackintosh full-length coat or cloak made of waterproof rubberized material

Jean Passepartout and Phileas Fogg in a television adaptation of the novel

Learning tip

Almost anything that can be revealed about a character can be presented via **dialogue**. It could be by what the character says himself/ herself, or by the dialogue of another character.

Pay attention to the power dynamics between the two main characters in this extract.

- Examine how a writer's use of language and grammatical features creates effect and meaning
- Consider the influence of literature from different historical periods

"Good! Take this carpet-bag," handing it back to Passepartout. "Take good care of it, for there are twenty thousand pounds in it."

60 Two first-class tickets for Paris having been speedily purchased, Mr. Fogg was crossing the station to the train, when he saw his five friends from the Reform Club.

"Well, gentlemen," said he, "I'm off, you see; and, if you will examine my passport when I get back, you will be able to judge

65 whether I have accomplished the journey agreed upon."

"Oh, that would be quite unnecessary, Mr. Fogg," said Ralph politely. "We will trust your word, as a gentleman of honour."

"You do not forget when you are due in London again?" asked Stuart.

70 "In eighty days; on Saturday, the 21st of December, 1872, at a quarter before nine p.m. Good-bye, gentlemen."

Phileas Fogg and his servant seated themselves in a first-class carriage at twenty minutes before nine; five minutes later the whistle screamed, and the train slowly glided out of the station.

75 The night was dark, and a fine, steady rain was falling. Phileas Fogg, snugly sitting in his corner, did not open his lips. Passepartout, not yet recovered from the shock of it all, clung mechanically to the carpet-bag, with its enormous treasure.

Just as the train was whirling through Sydenham, Passepartout
80 suddenly uttered a cry of despair.

"What's the matter?" asked Mr. Fogg.

"Alas! In my hurry – I – I forgot –"

"What?"

"To turn off the gas in my room!"

85 "Very well, young man," returned Mr. Fogg, coolly, "it will burn – at your expense."

From *Around the World in Eighty Days* by JULES VERNE

Language tip

The **semicolon** is used to join related but independent clauses together. To test whether you're using a semicolon correctly, you should be able to replace it with either a full stop or the word 'and'.

For example: 'I am here; you are there'.

You can also use the semicolon to separate items in a list if the items are long or contain internal punctuation.

For example: 'On her most recent trip, she travelled to Madrid and Barcelona, Spain; Rome and Florence, Italy; and Istanbul, Turkey.'

Comprehension

1 What is Phileas Fogg guilty of in the eyes of Passepartout?
2 Find the phrases that state what Passepartout expected of life with his new employer.
3 Describe Fogg's mood as he tells Passepartout his plans.
4 What essential items does Fogg take with him on his journey?
5 What did Passepartout forget, and how does his employer respond?

1 In what ways is Fogg a caricature of an English gentleman? Find examples in the text that reveal these characteristics.
2 How does the way Phileas Fogg and Passepartout are addressed or referred to in the text show their contrasting levels of privilege and social standing?
3 Write down your own insights into the grammar, typography, vocabulary and style of writing that places this text in the nineteenth century and not in the twenty-first century.

1 Which destinations would you choose on a round-the-world trip?
2 How would you go about planning and booking your travel and accommodation?
3 What differences would there be between planning and taking a round-the-world trip today and in the nineteenth century, like Jules Verne's characters?

- Explain how an author develops characters, setting and plot
- Use inference and deduction to find evidence in a text about the environment, culture and social situation

Given that it is now much quicker to travel around the world than in the 1800s, what travel-related challenge could you set today?

Stretch zone

Think of all the different words you can use to describe travel (for example, a trip, a journey) and the person travelling (for example, a journeyman, an adventurer).

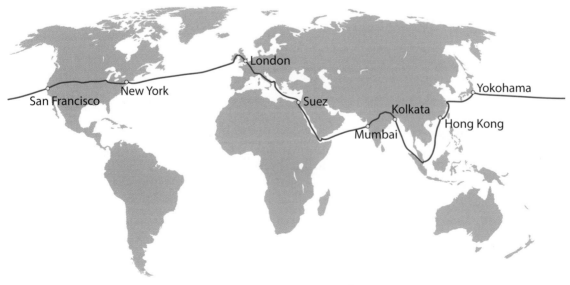

The route taken by Phileas Fogg in *Around the World in Eighty Days*

Travel writing: a real-life adventure

In 1873, Isabella Bird, an adventurer from England, rode a horse 800 miles through the Rocky Mountains in the western United States. She wrote letters home to her sister. Magazines and newspapers in England and the United States began buying these letters and publishing them, which provided her with money to continue travelling.

- Examine and discuss a wide range of texts with understanding and confidence
- Consider the influence of literature from different historical periods

Finding our way through the dark

After riding twenty miles, which made the distance for that day fifty, I remounted Birdie to ride six miles farther, to a house which had been mentioned to me as a stopping-place. The road rose to a height of 11,000 feet, and from thence I
5 looked my last at the lonely, uplifted prairie sea. 'Denver stage-road!' The worst, rudest, dismallest, darkest road I have yet travelled on, nothing but a winding ravine, the Platte Canyon, pine-crowded and pine-darkened, walled in on both sides for six
10 miles by pine-skirted mountains 12,000 feet high! Along this abyss for forty miles there are said to be only five houses, and were it not for miners going down, and freight-waggons going up, the solitude would be awful. As it was, I did not see
15 a creature. It was four when I left South Park, and between those mountain walls and under the pines it soon became quite dark, a darkness which could be felt. The snow which had melted in the sun had refrozen, and was one sheet of smooth
20 ice. Birdie slipped so alarmingly that I got off and walked, but then neither of us could keep our feet, and in the darkness she seemed so likely to fall upon me, that I took out of my pack the man's socks which had been given me at Perry's
25 Park, and drew them on over her fore-feet – a solution which for a time succeeded admirably, and which I suggested to all travellers similarly circumstanced. It was unutterably dark, and

- Examine how a writer's use of language and grammatical features creates effect and meaning
- Discuss ideas with others, questioning and evaluating opposing views

30 all these operations had to be performed by the sense of touch only. I remounted, allowed her to take her own way, as I could not see even her ears, and though her hind legs slipped badly, we managed to get along through the narrowest part of the canyon, with a tumbling river close to the road. The pines were very dense, and sighed and creaked mournfully in the severe 35 frost, and there were other eerie noises not easy to explain. At last, when the socks were nearly worn out, I saw the blaze of a campfire, with the two hunters sitting by it, on the hillside, and at the mouth of a gulch something which looked like buildings. We got across the river partly on ice and partly by 40 fording, and I found the place where I had been told that I could put up.

From *A Lady's Life in the Rocky Mountains* by ISABELLA BIRD

Glossary

ravine deep, narrow gorge or valley

abyss extremely deep pit

gulch North-American word for **ravine**

ford shallow part of the river that people or animals can walk across

Comprehension

1 Describe the characteristics of the landscape along the route.
2 How long do you think the journey takes that Isabella describes?
3 How do you know the writer is proud of her survival skills?
4 How can you tell that she has great affection for her horse?

1 What do you think the writer means by 'a darkness which could be felt'? (lines 17–18)
2 Find the adverb later in the extract that also reflects on the quality of the darkness and explain its meaning.
3 What poetic technique does the writer use to describe the sounds she hears? Explain its effect.
4 Find the sentence with multiple superlatives. How does this sentence sum up the qualities of the environment?

1 Where do you think Isabella Bird got the information from to prepare her for the journey?
2 Why do you think Isabella Bird's travel writing was popular?
3 Do you think travelling alone, just with a horse, across such dangerous terrain is a sensible idea?
4 How has technology made travelling safer today than in the 1800s?

Language tip
Adverbs add information and description to other words and often end in -*ly*. They answer questions like 'When?', 'Where?', 'Why?', 'How?' and 'How much?'

Language tip
Superlative adjectives are used to describe extremes. Look back at page 14 to remind yourself of how they are formed.

- Identify evidence in a text about the environment, culture and social situation

A different approach to travel writing

In this example of local travel, which might also be regarded as a spoof or satire of travel writing, the writer Michael Clerizo takes on the challenge of spending 24 hours at Heathrow Airport, treating it as one might a regular tourist destination.

Airport tourism

Want to make your friends laugh? Tell them you're spending 24 hours at an airport. Want to make your friends jealous? Tell them you're spending time away from workaday cares and responsibilities, exploring places, observing people and
5 indulging your inner child. In other words, tell them about the 24 hours you spent at an airport.

Epiphanies are difficult to define and their occurrence is always unpredictable. I'm not sure I've ever experienced one. But trundling along on the Piccadilly Line towards Heathrow
10 Airport, the site of my 24-hour visit, a sense of liberation washed over me.

Unlike my previous journeys, I had not once glanced anxiously at my watch. Time didn't matter. Nor had I constantly performed my usual nervous ritual of fumbling through my pockets,
15 making sure I had my passport, ticket and credit cards. All that was for people who were actually going somewhere. Me, I was just going to hang out. I didn't even have my passport with me – just a toothbrush, toothpaste, lots of stuff to read, a notebook and several pens.

20 7 am. I arrive at Terminal 4 and head for the airport information desk to pick up a few basic facts. I learn that the first flights land at around 5 am and the last arrive at 11 pm. The airport itself and some of the shops in the check-in and arrivals area never closed, but the trains that run between Terminal 4 and
25 Terminals 1, 2 and 3 stop at 11.45 pm. A helpful staff member advises me to spend the night in Terminals 1, 2 or 3 because they are bigger and livelier than Terminal 4 after hours.

As Douglas Adams observed in *The Long Dark Tea-Time of the Soul*, 'It can hardly be a coincidence that no language on
30 earth has ever produced the expression, "As pretty as an airport".' My plan is to pass some of my 24 hours searching for something 'pretty'.

Learning tip
In-text references can reveal a writer's influences and sources. Douglas Adams (referred to in line 28) is best known for the mock science-fiction series *The Hitchhiker's Guide to the Galaxy*. He is a well-known satirist of contemporary life.

Glossary

workaday ordinary, not unusual, or interesting
epiphany moment of sudden revelation or insight
Piccadilly Line a London Underground train line
mellower kinder or more sympathetic with age
invigorating providing strength or courage
virtuoso person with outstanding skill

Learning tip
Satire is the use of humour or exaggeration in order to criticize or ridicule aspects of human nature. Often it is a broader comment on a social group or custom.

• Examine how a writer's use of language and grammatical features creates effect and meaning

My personal vote for the prettiest site at Heathrow is the entry/exit ramp that wraps around the Short Stay Car Park 1. Built
35 from concrete and bricks, the sweeping curve of the ramp is as pretty as any French château staircase.

12.30 pm. Heathrow is a big, rambling place, and finding the ramp took four hours. It's time for lunch. Lunch is followed by a long stint of reading …

40 4 pm. I'm wandering around again when I have my second epiphany. "What an idiot I am!" (I'm sure the best epiphanies always begin with that thought.) An airport is a superb place for watching the world come and go. After all, that's exactly what the world is doing at an airport. Except for me – I'm
45 staying put for 24 hours.

I survey all four terminals and conclude that check-in areas are crowded, noisy and full of stress. Arrivals areas are mellower. Terminal 2 has a few rows of comfortable seats overlooking its arrival area. I sit and observe as people embrace, kiss, cry or yell
50 down their mobile phones: "I'm here, stupid – where are you?"

8 pm. Hanging around at Heathrow is like staying home from school and spending the entire day in your pajamas lying on the couch, watching TV and eating ice cream. (I can't think why it isn't more popular!)

55 12.15 am. At a little after midnight, the show ends. As the food shops close, I stock up on provisions for the night. Inside a display case, I see an example of East meeting West – the last doughnut is sitting next to an onion bhaji. I haggle and get the doughnut at half-price.

Language tip
We use **comparative adjectives** to say that one person or thing is of a higher quality or is a better example than another. We add the suffix -er to the adjective. Words like 'taller', 'smarter' and 'slower' are examples of comparative adjectives.

60 2 am. I feel sleepy. Hoping for an invigorating sugar rush, I eat the doughnut. It tastes of onion bhaji. Still sleepy, I decide to try some physical exercise: namely, pushing a baggage trolley through the tunnels that connect Terminals 1, 2 and 3. Each
65 tunnel has two moving walkways separated by an expanse of polished marble tiles.

While navigating the trolley on the tiles, the child in me takes over. Holding onto the trolley, I break into a run. I realize that I am reliving a game I played years ago in shopping-mall parking lots. I haven't lost my touch either, because I am still able to
70 judge the best moment to jump onto the back of the trolley and coast to a gentle stop.

2.45 am. Like all kids having fun, I attract the attention of others. A honeymoon couple from Texas, Brad and Amy, who have missed a connecting flight to Italy, have a few goes. We
75 play until two cleaners appear and we have to stop. I suggest that we move to another tunnel and try some floor skating. To floor skate, you remove your shoes and then break into a slide. Amy turns out to be a floor-skating virtuoso; she can even slide backwards.

80 4.15 am. We repair to one of the open-all-hours coffee shops for a caffeine hit. Brad, Amy and I chat for a while and then I make my way to the arrivals area in Terminal 3 to watch the people on the first flight from Hong Kong come in.

Back on the Piccadilly Line, I experience the perfect ending to
85 my 24-hour experiment. I fall asleep.

From *The Lonely Planet Guide to Experimental Travel*

Writing about a day in your life

Write an account of a day in your life when you experienced something out of the ordinary. Your account can be a real or imagined experience.

- Choose a particular place, social group or activity.
- Did you have a particular goal or plan that you set for yourself?
- What did you learn from the experience? Did you have an epiphany?
- Share your writing with a partner and offer each other feedback.

- Write a range of non-fiction texts, including autobiographies and letters
- Make sure text type, structure and style are suitable for intended audience
- Use punctuation to reflect characters' thoughts and feelings

Comprehension

1 How do we know that this extract is a satire?
2 Who and what is the writer satirizing?
3 How does he compare this experience to previous journeys?
4 Why is it important for him to find 'something pretty'?

1 Explain the writer's use of the following expressions, and how he uses them to further the narrative:
   a 'to have an epiphany' (lines 40–41)
   b 'watching the world come and go' (line 43)
   c 'an example of East meeting West' (line 57)
2 Find examples of comparative adjectives.

1 How does this 24-hour experiment portray the feelings and experiences that are usually associated with being at an airport?
2 How do you think the experiment has changed the writer's opinion of airports and travelling?

London Underground: 'The way for all'

The London Underground (or the 'Tube') has a long tradition of commissioning memorable advertising posters. In 2013, an exhibition of 150 of the best poster designs went on view in the London Transport Museum, including posters which:

- show how quickly and efficiently people can travel around London by Tube
- promote Tube travel to London's cultural spots like museums, galleries and gardens, and activities such as shopping, sports and theatre
- remind Londoners of the countryside just a train journey away.

Look at the posters on this page with a partner. Which do you think is the most effective and why? Talk about the use of text, images and colour to justify your opinion.

Learning tip
Search the collection on the Museum of Transport website for more examples of London Underground posters. What styles work best?

BRIGHTEST LONDON
IS BEST REACHED BY
UNDERGROUND

FOR THE ZOO, BOOK
TO REGENT'S PARK
OR CAMDEN TOWN
UNDERGROUND

THEATRELAND

TRAVEL BY UNDERGROUND
THERE ARE STATIONS WITHIN EASY
DISTANCE OF ALL THE THEATRES –
THERE ARE LATE TRAINS HOME IN
ALL DIRECTIONS –
THE SUREST & QUICKEST WAY
FROM & TO HOME.

WHITSUNTIDE OUTINGS
"SPRING IS ON THE WING"
SEEK IT BY BUS TRAM
OR UNDERGROUND

Promote your city!

Now it's your turn! Design a poster promoting a particular city, town or region that you know well. You could also do some research into a city which you would like to get to know, and promote that. Focus on the landmarks and features that make the place you have chosen distinctive and attractive.

- Choose which aspects of your city, town or region you want to focus on. Remember that limiting the content on a poster can often create greater impact.
- Consider text you will use on the poster. Choose a few key words or phrases.
- Be bold and creative with the title, graphics, colours and style to create a striking image.
- Include the modes of transport and other forms of recreation appropriate to this location. Make it look like people are enjoying themselves or having an adventure!

Write a text to accompany your poster and give a short presentation to your partner or group. Ask them to give you feedback on your ideas.

- Select the most appropriate media to deliver presentations, including photography and graphic artworks
- Participate fully in discussions

Talk about ...
- In what other ways do you experience advertising?
- How do you think advertising has changed from the early twentieth century to today?

Table Mountain, Cape Town

Singapore Flyer, Singapore

Casa Rosada, Buenos Aires

- Read and compare non-fiction texts and discuss their features

Newspaper article

Life is an adventure, but sometimes things go wrong. In this short newspaper article, written by reporter Bonnie Malkin, we get an insight into the risks of travel, and the sometimes flawed decisions a person makes in the heat of the moment.

Tourist feared he would die clinging to outback train

An American tourist has told how he feared he would die as he spent two and a half hours clinging to the outside of a train travelling through the Australian outback at speeds of up to 70 mph.

5 Chad Vance, a 19-year-old student from Alaska, jumped on to the Ghan, which travels from Adelaide to Darwin, as it pulled out of Port Augusta. He had hopped off to stretch his legs during a stop, and panicked when he saw it moving
10 off. He managed to squeeze into a small stairwell, but as the train gathered speed and night fell he realized his decision could be fatal.

"I was worried I wasn't going to survive," he said. "If I'd fallen off at that speed and hit the nasty-looking rocks
15 below, I don't think I would have made it." He clung on for two hours and 20 minutes before Marty Wells, a crew member, heard his cries for help and brought the train to an emergency stop. "Chad is a very lucky guy. When we rescued him, his skin was white and his lips were blue," Mr Wells told a newspaper.
20 "We were still about three hours away from our next scheduled stop, and in that time he could have easily died of hypothermia or lost his grip."

Mr Vance boarded the Ghan in Adelaide on 28 May for the journey to Alice Springs. He lost track of time in Port Augusta
25 and arrived back at the platform as the train was moving off. He said he knew it would pull up outside to change drivers, so he decided to chase it. When he caught it up, he banged on the windows of the first-class dining carriage. The passengers ignored him because they "probably thought I was some crazy
30 kid," he said.

Glossary

the Ghan train between Adelaide and Darwin that travels through central Australia; named after the original camel train and handlers who originally came from Afghanistan

hypothermia condition of having an abnormally low body temperature

After five minutes, the train started to pull away again and he made the "instinctive" decision, which he admitted was a "pretty crazy idea", to climb back on board. Wearing only jeans, boots and a t-shirt, he endured freezing temperatures
35 before he was rescued.

"He was shaking uncontrollably for several hours and complained of numbness to the left side of his body and arms and said his face was also stinging," Mr Wells said. "I've never seen anything like this before, and I sure hope I don't ever see it again."

From the DAILY TELEGRAPH, Sydney

- Explain how choosing certain language can enhance impact of writing
- Present personal opinions clearly and succinctly with confidence
- Discuss writing and spoken language with accurate use of linguistic terminology

Comprehension

1 What did Chad do that put his life at risk?
2 Why were the rocks below 'nasty-looking'? (line 14)
3 Why did the passengers in the dining car ignore him?
4 What is an 'instinctive' decision? (line 32)

B

1 Test your understanding of some common phrases. Find the words used to describe:
   a move or walk around
   b a train arriving at or departing from a station
   c putting up with a very cold temperature
   d an automatic response
2 **a** List the effects of shock and exposure that Chad experiences.
   b Which medical term is used to describe a condition that could have killed him?

C

1 This news article recounts an experience that you often read about in action or adventure stories or see on film. How different is the experience narrated from real life to one that we are more likely to associate with action heroes on the big screen?
2 Do you think it is a worthwhile news item for a national newspaper to report on?

Talk about …

Have you ever made a wrong decision? If so, how did you put things rights and what did you learn from the experience?

 Stretch zone

Write a letter or email to the newspaper in response to the article on Chad Vance, expressing your opinion on his actions.

Do you think he was extremely courageous, or incredibly foolish? Consider your tone, register and choice of language.

- Examine closely how texts mirror the time and place in which they are written

Moon fiction

The following extract from the science fiction novel *A Fall of Moondust* by Arthur C. Clarke describes a day trip on the Moon in the late twenty-first century. Published in 1961, just as the Russian astronaut Yuri Gagarin became the first person to fly in space, it predicted that humans would soon be colonizing other planets, starting with Earth's own moon.

A day trip on the Moon

To be the skipper of the only boat on the Moon was a distinction that Pat Harris enjoyed. As the passengers filed aboard Selene, jockeying for window seats, he wondered what sort of trip it would be this time. In the rear-view mirror he could see Miss
5   Wilkins, very smart in her blue Lunar Tourist Commission uniform, putting on her usual welcome act.

There were no familiar faces; this was a new bunch, eager for their first cruise. Most of the passengers were typical tourists – elderly people, visiting a world that had been the very symbol
10   of inaccessibility when they were young. There were only four or five passengers on the low side of thirty, and they were probably technical personnel on vacation from one of the lunar bases. It was a fairly good working rule, Pat had discovered, that all the old people came from Earth, while the youngsters
15   were residents of the Moon.

But to all of them, the Sea of Thirst was a novelty. Beyond Selene's observation windows, its gray, dusty surface marched onward unbroken until it reached the stars. Above it hung the waning crescent Earth, poised forever in the sky from which
20   it had not moved in a billion years. The brilliant, blue-green light of the mother world flooded this strange land with a cold radiance – and cold it was indeed, perhaps three hundred below zero on the old exposed surface.

No one could have told, merely by looking at it, whether the
25   Sea was liquid or solid. It was completely flat and featureless, quite free from myriad cracks and fissures that scarred all the rest of this barren world. Not a single hillock, boulder or pebble broke its monotonous uniformity. No sea on Earth – no millpond, even – was ever as calm as this.

30   It was a sea of dust, not of water, and therefore it was alien to

• Examine closely how texts mirror the time and place in which they are written

all the experiences of men; therefore, also, it fascinated and attracted them. Fine as talcum powder, drier in this vacuum than the parched sands of the Sahara, it flowed as easily and effortlessly as any liquid. A heavy object dropped into it would

35 disappear instantly, without a splash, leaving no scar to mark its passage. Nothing could move upon its treacherous surface except the small, two-man dust-skis – and Selene herself, an improbable combination of sledge and bus, not unlike the Sno-cats that had opened up the Antarctic a lifetime ago.

40 Selene's official designation was Dust-Cruiser, Mark I, though to the best of Pat's knowledge, a Mark II did not exist even on the drawing board. She was called 'ship', 'boat' or 'moon bus' according to taste; Pat preferred 'boat', for it prevented confusion. When he used that word, no one would mistake him for the skipper of

45 a spaceship – and spaceship captains were, of course, two a penny.

"Welcome aboard Selene," said Miss Wilkins, when everyone had settled down. "Captain Harris and I are pleased to have you with us. Our trip will last four hours, and our first objective will be Crater Lake, a hundred kilometres east of here, in the

50 Mountains of Inaccessibility."

Pat scarcely heard the familiar introduction; he was busy with his countdown. Oxygen OK. Power OK. Radio OK. ("Hello, Rainbow Base, Selene testing. Are you receiving my beacon?") Inertial navigator – zeroed. Air-lock safety – On. Cabin-leak

55 detector OK. Internal lights OK. Gangway disconnected. And so on for more than fifty items, every one of which would automatically call attention to itself in case of trouble. But Pat Harris, like all spacemen hankering after old age, never relied on auto-warnings if he could carry out the checks himself.

60 At last he was ready. The almost silent motors started to spin, but the blades were still feathered, and Selene barely quivered at her moorings. Then he eased the port fan into fine pitch, and she began to curve slowly to the right. When she was clear of the embarkation building, he straightened her out and pushed

65 the throttle forward.

She handled very well, when one considered the complete novelty of her design. There had been no millennia of trial and error here, stretching back to the first Neolithic man who ever launched a log out into a stream. Selene was the very first of

Glossary

skipper captain of a ship or team

to jockey to perform skilful moves and get a good position

inaccessible not accessible or easy to approach

hankering after longing for something

embarkation process of boarding a vehicle

throttle device that controls the flow of fuel to an engine

- Read a variety of texts and evaluate how writers develop ideas and themes in their writing
- Discuss the meaning of new and unfamiliar words
- Examine and discuss a wide range of texts
- Look at a variety of texts and evaluate how writers develop ideas and themes in their writing

70 her line. As they drilled through the dust, driving her before them, they produced a wake like that of a high-speed mole, but it vanished within seconds, leaving the Sea unmarked by any sign of the boat's passage.

Now the squat pressure-domes of Port Roris were dropped swiftly 75 below the skyline. In less than ten minutes, they had vanished from sight: Selene was utterly alone. She was at the centre of something for which the languages of mankind have no name.

As Pat switched off the motors and the boat coasted to rest, he waited for the silence to grow around him. It was always 80 the same; it took a little while for the passengers to realize the strangeness of what lay outside. They had crossed space and seen stars all about them; they had looked up – or down – at the dazzling face of Earth, but this was different. It was neither land nor sea, neither air nor space, but a little of each.

From *A Fall of Moondust* by Arthur C. Clarke

Glossary

Neolithic later Stone Age or New Stone Age
wake track left by a ship or other object moving in the water

Comprehension

A

1 From whose perspective is this extract from the novel written?
2 Who are the typical passengers on the cruise ship, and how many of them are local?
3 What are the key stops and locations on the tour?
4 Why is the Sea of Thirst a novelty?

B

1 Write the meaning of the following phrases from this extract:
   a 'spaceship captains were, of course, two a penny' (line 45)
   b 'all spacemen hankering after old age' (line 58)
   c 'no millennia of trial and error here' (lines 67–68)
   d 'a wake like that of a high-speed mole' (line 71)
2 Find examples in the text of stem words whose meaning is altered with the addition of a prefix such as *dis-*, *in-* or *un-*.

C

1 How does this extract reflect the experience of life in the mid-twentieth century and anticipate the new realities of the twenty-first century?

Language tip
Adding the prefixes *dis-*, *in-* or *un-* to a word is like putting 'not' in front of it to describe its opposite. For example: 'disjointed', 'inaccessible', 'unknown'.

Welcome to Galaxy Tours!

You are the lead tour guide for an inter-planetary travel company. Your team is about to take a group of tourists from Earth on an outer-space tour.

Write a script for your welcome address to the tourists.

- Start by introducing yourself and the rest of the crew, and explain the form of transport you are using. Think of a good opening point to capture the attention of the audience immediately and get them excited about the tour.
- Provide details of the tour itinerary, how long it will take, the places they will visit and the tour highlights.
- Include some background information about the geography, the wildlife and the inhabitants of the areas they will visit.
- Cover all the important information about the safety procedures, accommodation, food services (what's on the menu) and recreation facilities.

Come up with your own branding and key selling points.

Once you have finished your draft preparation, present your speech to the group and ask for feedback.

- Adapt writing style and register for intended audience and purpose
- Make sure text type, structure and style are suitable for the audience
- Write a science fiction script with confidence and creativity

Businesses are investing huge amounts of money into developing space tourism, but it still remains something only the very wealthiest can afford. Is this fair? Do you think we all deserve the opportunity to travel into space?

Stretch zone

Come up with your own logo design and poster to promote your inter-planetary tour.

Why is education so important?

Talk about ...
- What is a good education?
- How important is learning at all stages of life?
- How do we value education in a changing world?

> ' Learning is a treasure that will follow its owner everywhere. '
>
> Chinese proverb

There are many different stages or types of education that contribute to lifelong learning. It is generally considered an advantage to have the opportunity to go to school and get a formal education from early childhood. As you progress through this unit, consider all the different approaches to education, skills development and personal growth.

Word origins

education (n), comes from the Latin words *educare*, meaning 'to bring up', or 'train', and *educere*, meaning 'to lead out'

Related words:
- educator
- educational
- uneducated

Talking to a US president

In the following interview with the former US President Barack Obama, 11-year-old Damon Weaver from Pahokee in Florida takes the opportunity to raise issues that are close to his heart. The interview took place in 2009, around the time when the president was due to make a statement on his government's education policies.

Weaver had already interviewed a number of prominent people in the United States. Pay attention to his interview techniques.

* Identify facts, opinions and viewpoints
* Use the grammar and vocabulary of formal and informal registers
* Discuss reading, writing and spoken language

An interview with President Obama

DAMON WEAVER: I've heard that you would like to make an announcement about education. Can you tell me about the announcement?

PRESIDENT OBAMA: Well, Damon, on September 8,
5 when young people around the country have just started or are about to go back to school, I'm going to be making a big speech to people all across the country about the importance of education and the importance of staying in school, about how we want to improve the education system and why it's
10 so important for the country, so I hope everybody tunes in.

WEAVER: All across America, money is being cut from education. How can education be improved with all these cuts?

President Obama and Damon Weaver

OBAMA: Well, we here in the administration are actually trying to
15 put more money into schools, and there are a lot of schools all across the country that are getting new buildings and new facilities. We're now putting more money into training good teachers and giving them more support. But money alone is not going to make the difference. We've also got to improve how the schools are
20 operating, and we have been trying to focus on how you identify the best schools and figure out what it is that they're doing well. And we're trying to get other schools that aren't doing so well to do the same kinds of things that the schools who are doing well are doing. So I hope that we can really see some improvement, not just with
25 funding, but also with reforming how the schools work.

Can I also add that there are certain programs, like dropout prevention programs, for example, that local school districts might not be able to afford, but we can provide federal government funding to those local districts so they can support such programs.

Language tip

Notice that 'education' and 'administration' share the same suffix.

-*tion* is a suffix occurring in words of Latin origin used to form **abstract nouns** that express an action, state or condition.

- Identify facts, opinions and viewpoints
- Use the grammar and vocabulary of formal and informal registers
- Discuss reading, writing and spoken language

30 **WEAVER:** I've learned that your mom always made sure that you were doing well at school. What should parents do to make sure their child's education is better?

OBAMA: Parents are the most important thing to any child's ability to do well in school, so making sure you're reading to your children, 35 especially when they're young, even before they get to school so they start being used to reading, and they know their alphabet, they know the basics. So even when they get to kindergarten, they're already a leg up. I think it's important to make sure that kids are doing their homework and that they're not just turning on the TV all day or playing 40 video games. I think parents should talk to teachers and find out from teachers directly what can be done to improve their child's performance. Setting a high standard is also important. Saying if you get a B, you can do better, you can get an A. Making sure we have high expectations for all children because I think all children can do well, as long as they 45 have the support that they need. [...]

WEAVER: What can kids do to make our country better?

OBAMA: I think the things that kids can do best is just work really hard in school and succeed. If young people like yourself are reading at high levels, doing their homework, doing math and science and 50 ending up going to college, that makes everyone better off. But also when they have some spare time, try to help people out. It could be people in your church or your religious community, or out in the neighborhood. Helping an elderly person carry their grocery bags or helping out a younger person with their schoolwork, those kind of 55 things are also really helpful to the country.

Talk about ...

You may notice some American English spellings in this text, such as 'mom', 'math' and 'neighborhood'.

- What are the British English equivalents of these?
- What other words can you think of with American English spelling?

Glossary

facility building or piece of equipment; also used to describe a particular skill in doing something

reforming making changes to improve someone or something

performance the way in which someone does something or the standard they reach

constructive helpful and positive

homeboy boy or man from a person's local neighbourhood

outstanding extremely good, also a debt or bill to be paid

Damon Weaver in Pahokee, Palm Beach County, Florida

- Identify facts, opinions and viewpoints
- Use the grammar and vocabulary of formal and informal registers
- Discuss reading, writing and spoken language

WEAVER: Everybody knows that you love basketball. I think it would be cool to have a president who could dunk. Can you dunk?

OBAMA: Not anymore. I used to when I was young, but I'm almost 50 now. Your legs are the first thing to go!

60   **WEAVER:** My buddy Dwayne Wade promised me if you gave me the interview he would play you in a one-on-one basketball game. But he's not sure if he would let you score. Would you be willing to play him in a one-on-one basketball game?

OBAMA: I would play Dwayne Wade. I've got to admit, though, 65   Dwayne Wade is a little bit better at basketball than I am, so I would rather have him on my team playing against someone else than play against him.

WEAVER: What is it like to be President of the United States?

OBAMA: Well, it's very exciting, it's a lot of work, and there are 70   times where you get a little worn down. But every day you have the possibility, the ability to help other people, and if you can do that, it's a great, great thing.

WEAVER: In my town, Pahokee, I've seen a lot of shootings and fights. What are you going to do about violence and to keep me safe?

75   **OBAMA:** Well, I think that we have to make sure that all schools have resources to keep kids safe, but also that parents and community members participate in training their young people to resolve arguments and disagreements without resorting to violence. Too many of our young people, they get frustrated or angry with each other, they start 80   acting out in violence. We need to make sure that we're teaching young people to deal with the issues that they may have in a better way, in a more constructive way.

WEAVER: I know that you're busy being the president, but I would like to invite you to my school, Canal Point Elementary School, because 85   there's a lot of good things going on there that I would like you to see.

OBAMA: Well I hope that at some point I get a chance to visit your school because you did a great job on this interview! So somebody must be doing something right down at that school.

WEAVER: When I interviewed Vice President Joe Biden, he became 90   my homeboy. Would you like to become my homeboy?

OBAMA: Absolutely, thank you man. Great job.

WEAVER: Thanks for making my dream come true, Mr President.

OBAMA: Well I appreciate it. You did an outstanding job. I look forward to seeing you in the future.

Learning tip

Sometimes words take on a meaning that is slightly different to the standard dictionary definition, so you may need to do some further research when working out the meaning.

An example is 'to dunk', meaning to dip something. Here it is a shortened form of the phrase 'slam dunk' used to describe the dramatic leap required to force the ball into the net in a game of basketball.

- Evaluate a different social situation
- Choose a viewpoint to write from
- Use an interview as a model for own writing
- Select the most appropriate form of media and multimedia elements to deliver presentations on a range of topics

Comprehension

1 What are the key issues that Damon Weaver raises?

2 Why do you think he chose those specific topics?

3 Choose one question and one reply. Explain why the issue is important and analyze the effectiveness of the question and answer.

4 What are the main points Barack Obama makes about educational values?

1 Focus on the interview technique of Weaver. Summarize his style and approach.

2 Look closely at Obama's language. Is there a pattern to his response to the questions?

3 Find other examples of words that conclude with the suffix -tion. Identify the verb stem used in each case.

4 Obama uses understatement when he says that Dwayne Wade (a former professional basketball player) is only 'a little bit better' at basketball than he is. (line 65) Why does he use understatement and what might it tell us about Obama's personality?

1 How successful do you think Weaver's interview is? Justify your answer.

2 Do you think the answers Obama gave Weaver were different to those he would have given an adult?

Preparing an interview

Prepare to do an interview for your school magazine or community radio about education. You could interview a parent, your teacher or school principal.

- Draft a list of possible questions and comments.
- Consider ways that you could add in some light relief and humour to put the person you are interviewing at ease. Take inspiration from Damon Weaver's interview techniques.
- Listen and respond politely, but don't be scared to ask difficult questions while being open to different viewpoints.

You could obtain your interviewee's permission and make an audio or video recording of the interview. Watch or listen to this afterwards to help you evaluate the success of your interview.

Stretch zone

Take your turn as the person being interviewed, and answer the question, 'What are the biggest challenges facing schools today?'

- Consider how poets play with different themes and conventions
- Write a range of different fiction genres and poetry

A poem about a reluctant student

The following poem is a humorous take on the barriers between the teacher and the student. Billy McBone appears to be uninspired and resistant to learning. But there can be two sides to the story.

Billy McBone

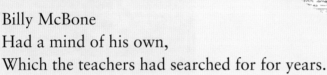

Billy McBone
Had a mind of his own,
Which he mostly kept under his hat.
The teachers all thought
5 That he couldn't be taught,
But Bill didn't seem to mind that.

Billy McBone
Had a mind of his own,
Which the teachers had searched for for years.
10 Trying test after test,
They still never guessed
It was hidden between his ears.

Billy McBone
Had a mind of his own,
15 Which only his friends ever saw.
When the teacher said, 'Bill,
Whereabouts is Brazil?'
He just shuffled and stared at the floor.

Billy McBone
20 Had a mind of his own,
Which he kept under lock and key.
While the teachers in vain
Tried to burgle his brain,
Bill's thoughts were off wandering free.

ALLAN AHLBERG

What's in a name?

Using the example of 'Billy McBone', write a poem focusing on the eponymous hero or heroine ('eponymous' means their name is in the title).

- Introduce a rhyme scheme, as in 'Billy McBone'.
- Use poetic techniques such as rhyming couplets, repetition and alliteration.
- Think of a dramatic or memorable way to finish your poem and read it out to your class or group for comments.

Comprehension

A

1 What is implied by the phrase 'a mind of his own'?
2 Who is to blame for Billy's refusal to learn? Choose lines to support your answer.

B

1 What type of rhyme scheme is used throughout the poem?
2 The first stanza of this poem sets out the style of all the stanzas in its use of rhyming phrases, repetition and alliteration. What effect does this approach have on the reader throughout the poem?

C

1 What comment about education do you think the poet is making?

A play about teaching methods

In his play *The History Boys,* the British playwright Alan Bennett focuses on a select group of students in their final years at school, who are being given special coaching to help them get a scholarship to one of the top universities in England. Bennett's exploration of teaching methods, however, is relevant to the experience of all students.

In the following selection of scenes from the play, various methods of teaching history and passing exams effectively are discussed among the teachers and students. Not everyone is in agreement. Mrs Lintott and Irwin are teachers. Dakin and Rudge are students.

- Develop ideas and themes gathered from a variety of texts
- Examine how a writer's use of language and grammatical features creates effect and meaning
- Perform playscripts with confidence and expression

Christ Church College at the University of Oxford

The History Boys

Staff room

	Headmaster	Mrs Lintott, Dorothy.
	Mrs Lintott	Headmaster?
	Headmaster	These Oxbridge boys. Your historians ...
5		Their A Levels are very good. And that is thanks to you, Dorothy. We've never had so many. Remarkable! But what now – in teaching terms?
	Mrs Lintott	More of the same?
	Headmaster	Oh, do you think so?
10	Mrs Lintott	It's what we've done before.
	Headmaster	Quite. Without much success. No one last year. When did we last have anyone in history at Oxford and Cambridge?

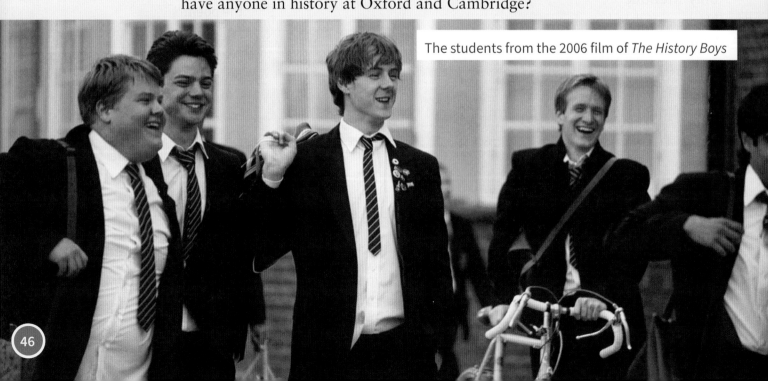
The students from the 2006 film of *The History Boys*

	Mrs Lintott	I tend not to distinguish.
	Headmaster	Between Oxford and Cambridge?
15	Mrs Lintott	Between centres of higher learning. Last year two at Bristol, one at York. The year before ...
	Headmaster	Yes, yes. I know that, Dorothy. But I am thinking league tables. Open scholarships. Reports to the Governors ... Factually tip-top as your boys always are, something more is required ... I would call it grooming did that not have overtones of the monkey house. 'Presentation' might be the word.
20		
	Mrs Lintott	They know their stuff. Plainly stated and properly organized facts need no presentation, surely.
25	Headmaster	Oh, Dorothy. I think they do. 'The facts: serving suggestion.'
	Mrs Lintott	A sprig of parsley, you mean?
	Headmaster	I am thinking of the boys. Clever, yes, remarkably so. Well taught. But a little ... *ordinaire*? Think charm. Think polish. Think Renaissance man.
30		
	Mrs Lintott	Yes, Headmaster.

School room

	Irwin	(*distributing exercise books*) Dull. Dull. Abysmally dull. A triumph ... the dullest of the lot.
35	Dakin	I got all the points.
	Irwin	I didn't say it was wrong.
		If you want to learn about Stalin, study Henry VIII. If you want to learn about Margaret Thatcher, study Henry VIII. The wrong end of the stick is the right one. A question has a front door and a back door. Go in the back, or better still, the side. Be perverse.
40		
45		Take Stalin. Generally agreed to be a monster, and rightly. Find something, anything, to say in his defence. History nowadays is not a matter of conviction. It's a performance. It's entertainment. And if it isn't, make it so.

- Develop ideas and themes gathered from a variety of texts
- Examine how a writer's use of language and grammatical features creates effect and meaning
- Perform playscripts with confidence and expression
- Understand the meaning and effect of new and unfamiliar words

Glossary

Oxbridge the universities of Oxford and Cambridge

A Level (Advanced Level) qualification in the UK used to qualify for university entrance

ordinaire French word for 'ordinary'

serving suggestion term used on food packaging to show ways to present food

Renaissance man a person who has attained high level of education across many disciplines

The teachers from the 2006 film

- Read a variety of texts and evaluate how writers develop ideas and themes in their writing
- Compare and contrast a wide range of texts on the same theme

50   **Rudge**   I get it. It's an angle. You want us to find an angle.

School corridor

50   **Mrs Lintott**   Ah, Rudge.

   Rudge   Miss.

   Mrs Lintott   How are you getting on with Mr Irwin?

   Rudge   It's … interesting Miss, if you know what I mean. It makes me grateful to you for your lessons.

55   **Mrs Lintott**   Really? That's nice to hear.

   Rudge   Firm foundations type thing. Point A. Point B. Point C. Mr Irwin is more … free-range.

   Mrs Lintott   I hadn't thought of you as a battery chicken, Rudge.

60   **Rudge**   It's only a metaphor, Miss.

   Mrs Lintott   I'm relieved to hear it.

   Rudge   You've force-fed us the facts; now we're in the process of running around acquiring flavour.

   Mrs Lintott   Is that what Mr Irwin says?

65   **Rudge**   Oh no, Miss. The metaphor's mine.

From *The History Boys* by ALAN BENNETT

Glossary

free-range farms that allow animals more space to move around and enjoy a varied diet and lifestyle

battery chicken form of intensive farming where chickens are confined to very small cages

Stretch zone

Write your own imagined dialogue as a 'history boy' or 'history girl', responding to the teacher's instructions at the bottom of page 47.

Comprehension

1 What is the headmaster's ultimate ambition for the 'history boys'?

2 How does Mrs Lintott disagree with the headmaster?

3 What is Mrs Lintott's view of a good education?

1 Rudge uses a metaphor to describe the difference between Mrs Lintott's and Mr Irwin's teaching styles. Explain the metaphor.

1 Based on the exchange of views in this extract from the play, what do you think is the best approach to learning history?

2 What impression do you get of Rudge? Do you think he will be successful in getting a scholarship to study history?

Learning to live

Much of what we learn is motivated by the challenges we encounter in daily life. The following extract is written by the philosopher and writer Alain de Botton, who founded The School of Life, which is an organization that helps teach people how to lead more fulfilled lives.

- Read a variety of texts and evaluate how writers develop ideas and themes in their writing

The School of Life

There is a deliberate paradox in the term 'the school of life'. School is meant to teach us what we need to know to live and yet, as the phrase suggests, it is most often life – by which we really mean painful experience – that does the bulk of the
5 instruction for us. The real institution called The School of Life therefore carries within it a hope and a provocation. It dares to believe that we might learn, in good time, what we might otherwise acquire only through many decades of stumbling. And it gently criticizes the current way we set about equipping
10 ourselves with the skills we need to thrive.

We aren't ever done with the odd business of becoming that most extraordinary and prized of things, an emotionally mature person – or, to put it a simpler way, an almost grown-up adult. In an ideal society, it would be not only children who were
15 known to need an education. All adults would recognize that they inevitably required continuing education of an emotional kind and would remain active followers of a psychological curriculum. Schools devoted to emotional intelligence would be open for everyone, so that children would feel that they
20 were participating in the early stages of a lifelong process. Some classes – about anger or sulking, blame or consideration – would have seven-year-olds learning alongside fifty-five-year-olds, the two cohorts having been found to have equivalent maturities in a given area. In such a society, the phrase 'I've finished school'
25 would sound extremely strange.

We have collectively left to chance some of what is most important to know; we have denied ourselves the opportunity to systematically transmit wisdom – reserving our belief in education to technical and managerial skills. The School of
30 Life is a modest attempt to try to spare us a bit of time.

From The School of Life: An Emotional Education by ALAIN DE BOTTON

The London branch of The School of Life

- Read a variety of texts and evaluate how writers develop ideas and themes in their writing
- Understand how a point of view is conveyed in a text

Comprehension

A

1 What is the 'deliberate paradox' central to the author's idea of 'the school of life'?

2 What field or area of study is mentioned that supports the focus on an emotional education?

3 In what way do adults and children often demonstrate an 'equivalent maturity'?

4 How does The School of Life propose to save us time?

B

1 Which point of view is the text written from?

2 What effect does this point of view give the text?

C

1 What are the bigger questions that this extract introduces about lifelong learning? Come up with some ideas to deal with the challenges.

Stretch zone

Imagine you are going to teach a class at The School of Life about being considerate. Note down some activities or discussion questions that would help your students learn and practise this skill.

Memories of childhood in South Africa

Nelson Mandela was born in 1918 in a village called Mvezo in the Eastern Cape of South Africa. He was the first person in his family to receive a formal education. Many years later he became the first-ever black president of South Africa. But before that, he endured 27 years in prison for his anti-government activities, and it was in prison that he began to write his autobiography from which the following extract is taken.

Traditional Xhosa huts in Qunu, where Mandela attended school

- Look at how texts are structured and presented in order to influence the reader's point of view

My early days

My home village of Qunu was situated in a narrow, grassy valley criss-crossed by clear streams, and overlooked by green hills. It consisted of no more than a few hundred people who lived in huts, which were beehive-shaped structures of mud
5   walls, holding up a peaked grass roof. [...]

From an early age, I spent most of my free time in the veld playing and fighting with the other boys of the village. At night, I shared my food and blanket with these same boys. I was no more than five when I became a herd-boy looking after sheep
10   and calves in the fields. I discovered the almost mystical attachment that the Xhosa have for cattle, not only as a source of wealth, but as a blessing and a source of happiness. It was in the fields that I learned how to knock birds out of the sky with a slingshot, to gather wild honey and fruits and edible
15   roots, to drink warm, sweet milk straight from the udder of a cow, to swim in the clear, cold streams, and to catch fish with string and sharpened bits of wire. From these days I date my love of the veld, of open spaces, the simple beauties of nature, the clean line of the horizon.

20   As boys, we were mostly left to our own devices. We played with toys we made ourselves. We moulded animals and birds out of clay. We made ox-drawn sledges out of tree branches. Nature was our playground. The hills above Qunu were dotted with large smooth rocks which we transformed into our own roller-
25   coaster. We sat on flat stones and slid down the face of the large rocks. I learned to ride by sitting on top of calves – after being thrown to the ground several times, one got the hang of it.

I learned my lesson one day from an unruly donkey. We had been taking turns climbing up and down its back and when
30   my chance came, I jumped on, and the donkey bolted into a nearby thorn bush. It bent its head, trying to unseat me, which it did, but not before the thorns had pricked and scratched my face, embarrassing me in front of my friends. Africans have a highly developed sense of dignity. I had lost face among my
35   friends. Even though it was a donkey that unseated me, I learned that to humiliate another person is to make him suffer an unnecessarily cruel fate. Even as a boy, I defeated my opponents without dishonouring them.

The Mbekela brothers would often see me playing or minding
40   sheep and come over to talk to me. One day, George Mbekela

Nelson Mandela at home in Qunu on his 90th birthday in 2008

Glossary

veld *(from the Dutch word for 'field')* unenclosed grassland country of South Africa

Xhosa African people whose traditional homeland is the Cape Provinces of South Africa

Mbekela brothers were from a different tribe and had received an education

Talk about ...

- What kind of truths do you think autobiographies reveal?

- Have you ever heard of the concept of an 'unreliable narrator'? Do you think this applies to autobiographies?

- Evaluate a different environment, culture and social situation
- Discuss the context and setting in which a story is written
- Write a range of non-fiction texts

45 paid a visit to my mother. "Your son is a clever young fellow," he said. "He should go to school." My mother remained silent. No one in my family had ever attended school and my mother was unprepared for Mbekela's suggestion. But she did relay it to my father who, despite – or perhaps because of – his own lack of education, immediately decided that his youngest son should go to school.

50 The schoolhouse consisted of a single room, with a Western-style roof, on the other side of the hill from Qunu. I was seven years old, and on the day before I was to begin, my father took me aside and told me that I must be dressed properly for school. Until that time, I, like all the other boys in Qunu, had worn only a blanket, which was wrapped round one shoulder and pinned at the waist. My father took a pair of his trousers and
55 cut them at the knee. He told me to put them on, which I did, and they were roughly the correct length, although the waist was far too large. My father then took a piece of string and drew the trousers in at the waist. I must have been a comical sight, but I have never owned a suit I was prouder to wear
60 than my father's cut-off trousers.

From *My Early Days* by NELSON MANDELA

Comprehension

1 Explain the 'mystical attachment' the Xhosa had for their cattle. (lines 10–11)
2 What did Mandela learn from the incident with the donkey?
3 What reason did Mandela's father give for agreeing to his son going to school?

1 What is meant by the following idiomatic phrases:
  a 'left to our own devices' (line 20)
  b 'Nature was our playground' (lines 22–23)
  c 'I had lost face'? (line 34)

1 What does the last sentence tell you about Mandela and his values?
2 How does Mandela's account of his boyhood support his leadership role in later life?

All about you!

You don't have to be famous to write an autobiography. Write a short account of a significant period in your early life. Write about what you did, and how you felt. Think about how those early memories have shaped the person you are today.

Stretch zone

Write a short summary of what fascinates you about real-life stories, and the useful perspectives that can be drawn from them.

A teacher's true story

E.R. Braithwaite was born in Georgetown, Guyana, and later immigrated to the UK, where he studied physics at Cambridge University. He worked in the 1950s as a teacher in the East End of London, where he struggled with his undisciplined class of final-year students who had little or no aspiration to higher learning.

One morning, in desperation, he tries to win their trust and cooperation by talking frankly about what he wants them to achieve together.

The teacher played by Sidney Poitier in the 1967 film *To Sir, with Love*

My plans for this class

"I would like you to listen to me without interrupting in any way, and when I'm through any one of you may say your piece without interruption from me." I was making it up as I went along and watching them; at the
5   least sign that it wouldn't work I'd drop it, fast.

They were interested, in spite of themselves; even the husky, blasé Denham was leaning forward on his desk watching me.

"My business here is to teach you, and I shall do my best to
10   make my teaching as interesting as possible. If at any time I say anything which you do not understand or with which you do not agree, I would be pleased if you would let me know. Most of you will be leaving school within six months or so; that means that in a short while you will be embarked on the
15   very adult business of earning a living. Bearing that in mind, I have decided that from now on you will be treated, not as children, but as young men and women, by me and by each other. When we move out of the state of childhood certain higher standards of conduct are expected of us ..."

20   At this moment the door was flung open and Pamela Dare rushed in, somewhat breathlessly, to take her seat. She was very late.

"For instance," I continued, "there are really two ways in which a person may enter a room; one is in a controlled, dignified
25   manner, the other is as if someone had just planted a heavy foot on your backside. Miss Dare has just shown us the second way; I'm quite sure she will now give us a demonstration of the first." [...]

- Read and discuss classic texts
- Find evidence about an environment, culture and social situation

30 All eyes were on her as she had probably planned, but instead of supporting her entrance they were watching her, waiting to see the result of my challenge. She blushed.

"Well, Miss Dare."

Her eyes were black with anger and humiliation, but she stood up and walked out, closing the door quietly behind her; then
35 to my surprise, and I must confess, my relief, she opened it as quietly, and with a grace and dignity that would have benefited a queen, she walked to her seat.

"Thank you. As from today there are certain courtesies which will be observed at all times in this classroom. Myself you will
40 address as 'Mr Braithwaite' or 'Sir' – the choice is yours; the young ladies will be addressed as 'Miss' and the young men will be addressed by their surnames."

I hadn't planned any of this, but it was unfolding all by itself, and I hoped, fitting into place. There was a general gasp at this,
45 from boys and girls alike.

Potter was the first to protest.

"Why should we call 'em 'Miss', we know 'em."

"What is your name?"

"Potter."

50 "I beg your pardon?"

"Potter, Sir." The 'Sir' was somewhat delayed.

"Thank you, Potter. Now is there any young lady present whom you consider unworthy of your courtesies?"

"Sir?"

55 "Is there any one of these young ladies, who you think does not deserve to be addressed as Miss?"

The girls all turned around to look at Potter, as if daring him; he drew back before their concerted eyes and said, "No, Sir."

"You should remember, Potter, that in a little while all of you
60 may be expected to express these courtesies as part of your jobs; it would be helpful to you to become accustomed to giving and receiving them."

Talk about …

- How important is it to learn to show respect to other people?
- Even if we use different language today to that used in the 1950s, do you think the principles of respect and courtesy are the same? What has changed?

Glossary

courtesies things a person does to be polite
concerted determined, usually as part of a group of similarly determined people

- Read and discuss classic texts
- Find evidence about an environment, culture and social situation

65 I walked around my desk and sat in my chair. For the time being at least they were listening, really listening to me; maybe they would not understand every word, but they'd get the general import of my remarks.

"The next point concerns the general deportment and conduct of the class. First, the young ladies. They must understand that in future they must show themselves both worthy and appreciative 70 of the courtesies we men will show them. [...]

"Now the boys. I have seen stevedores and longshoremen who looked a lot cleaner and tidier. There is nothing weak or unmanly about clean hands and faces, and shoes that are brushed. A man who is strong and tough never needs to show it in his 75 dress or the way he cuts his hair. Toughness is a quality of the mind, like bravery or honesty or ambition; it has nothing whatever to do with muscles. [...]

"You are the top class; the operative word is 'top'. That means you must set the standards in all things for the rest of the 80 school, for, whether you wish it or no, the younger ones will ape everything you do or say. They will try to walk like you and use the words you use, and dress like you, and so, for as long as you're here, much of their conduct will be your responsibility. [...] I shall help you in every way I can, both by 85 example and encouragement. I believe that you have it in you to be a fine class, the best this school has ever known, but I could be wrong; it all depends on you. Now any questions?"

From *To Sir With Love* by E.R. BRAITHWAITE

Glossary

deportment how a person moves and behaves in public

stevedores and **longshoremen** are employed to unload cargo from boats, that are stationed in docks or along a shoreline

ape imitate

Millwall Docks in East London, 1950s

Comprehension

1 What resistance is there at first to the teacher's plans?

2 How does he manage to capture the students' interest and attention?

3 What polite forms of address does the teacher suggest they use?

4 What lessons do the students learn?

5 What kind of example does the teacher want the class to set for the rest of the school? Why is this so important?

1 Explain the meaning of the following phrases and expressions:

   a 'interested, in spite of themselves' (line 6)

   b 'unworthy of your courtesies' (line 53)

   c 'the operative word' (line 78)

2 Consider the use of motivating language that the teacher uses in his address to the class. Write down three examples of strongly worded recommendations of behaviour or personal qualities that the teacher is suggesting the students should aspire to.

1 The author describes the moment he decides to put away the books and teach his final year students more useful life lessons. What does this extract reveal about the opportunities for students living in a low income area?

2 How relevant is this example from 1950s London to the challenges that many students throughout the world face today?

- Discuss writing and spoken language in order to convey ideas in detail
- Explain how language can enhance impact, create structure and contribute to the purpose of the text
- Use formal vocabulary to create an effect in writing

Talk about ...

- Do we ever stop learning?
- What other kinds of instruction or learning can you participate in that are not part of a school or university curriculum?

How important is the opportunity for an education? How different would your life be now if you didn't go to school or get an education?

Who are you inspired by?

Write about a teacher or mentor who has inspired you.

- What did they do to motivate you and win your respect? Use specific examples and explain how their words, attitude or behaviour impacted you.
- Pay attention to how their words of advice, recommendation, instruction or aspiration, as well as other examples of empowering language, had an impact on you.
- Discuss the person you chose and the reasons they inspired you with a partner. Do you find the same behaviour and language inspiring and empowering, or not?

4 Work

Why do we work?

> ❝ Work! work! work!
> While the cock is crowing aloof!
> And work – work – work,
> Till the stars shine through the roof! ❞
>
> From 'The Song of the Shirt' by THOMAS HOOD

Talk about ...

- Do people work just to earn money?
- How important to our lives is the work that we do?
- What kind of job do you think you would enjoy doing after you have completed your education?
- What do you think you would be good at?
- What might you find more challenging?

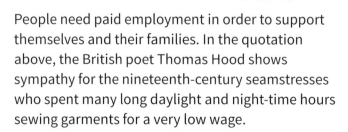

People need paid employment in order to support themselves and their families. In the quotation above, the British poet Thomas Hood shows sympathy for the nineteenth-century seamstresses who spent many long daylight and night-time hours sewing garments for a very low wage.

Think about the meaning and purpose of work as you go through this unit and read about different perspectives on working life.

Feeling the heat: a young chef's first job

Anthony Bourdain was an American celebrity chef turned writer. In the following extract from his autobiography *Kitchen Confidential*, he talks about getting his first real job after graduating. This behind-the-scenes account of a top New York restaurant provides a contemporary example of what it is like to work in an extremely pressured and over-heated environment.

The kitchen

On the strength of my diploma – and my willingness to work for peanuts – I landed a job almost right away at the venerable New York institution, the Rainbow Room,
5   high at the top of the Rockefeller Center. It was my first experience of the real Big Time, one of the biggest, busiest and best-known restaurants in the country. I was willing to do anything to prove myself, and
10 when I got in that elevator to the sixty-fourth-floor kitchen for the first time, I felt as if I was blasting off to the moon.

The Rainbow Room at that time sat a little over 200 people. The Rainbow Grill sat about another 150. Added to that were
15 two lounges where food was available, *and* an entire floor of banquet rooms – all of it serviced simultaneously by a single, central kitchen. So you had some major league volume, as well as some major league cooks to go along with it.

A long hot line of glowing flat-tops ran along one wall, flames
20 actually roaring back up into a fire wall behind them. A few feet across, separated by a narrow, trench-like workspace, ran an equally long stainless-steel counter. Much of this counter was taken up by vast, open steam boilers which were kept at a constant, rolling boil. What the cooks had to contend with
25 was a long, uninterrupted slot, with no air circulation, with nearly unbearable dry, radiant heat on one side and clouds of wet steam heat on the other. When I say unbearable, I mean they couldn't bear it; cooks would regularly pass out and have to be dragged off to recuperate.

Glossary

venerable worthy of respect or honour, especially because of great age

flat-tops cooking appliance with a flat, metal surface

contend with deal with something difficult

pass out faint

recuperate get better

inflame cause redness, heat or swelling (also to produce strong feelings)

30 There was so much heat coming off those ranges – especially when the center rings were lit for direct fire – that the filters in the overhead hoods would often burst into flames, inspiring a somewhat comical scene as the overweight Italian chef would hurl himself down the narrow line with a fire extinguisher,
35 bowling over the cooks and tripping as he hurried to put out the flames before the central system went off and filled the entire kitchen with fire-suppressant foam.

As I've said, it was hot. Ten minutes into the shift, the cheap polyester whites we all wore would be soaked through with
40 sweat, clinging to chest and back. All the cooks' necks and wrists were pink and inflamed with awful heat rashes. It was a madhouse.

From *Kitchen Confidential* by ANTHONY BOURDAIN

Language tip
UK or US language?
You have probably noticed already that British and American words and spelling can differ. An example is 'center', as in Rockefeller Center. The names of institutions and organizations must always be spelled in the original form.

- Examine how a writer's use of language and grammatical features creates effect and meaning
- Participate fully in discussions

Comprehension

A

1 What does 'work for peanuts' mean?

2 Why was the writer willing to 'work for peanuts'? (line 2)

3 What does he mean by 'the Big Time'? (lines 6–7)

4 What sporting term is used to describe the workload and experience of the other cooks?

5 In what ways were the working conditions literally 'unbearable'? (line 26)

6 What terrible outcome does the Italian chef's quick actions prevent?

B

1 Complete the following sentences by finding the best matching noun phrases from the text. (Hints are provided in brackets.)

| The boilers issued a wet (evaporation) _____. |
| His skin had become inflamed with a (red irritation) _____. |
| The oven released a (great warmth) _____. |
| She shielded her face from the (open fire) _____. |

2 Add appropriate prepositions that complete the following verb phrases. (There are additional prompts in brackets.)

| to blast _____ into space (in a rocket) |
| to pass _____ from exhaustion (to faint) |
| to burst _____ flames (to ignite) |
| to soak _____ his shirt (get completely wet) |
| to fill _____ smoke (to become very smoky) |
| to cling _____ for fear of falling (hold something or someone) |

C

1 What kind of expectation does the promise of a 'tell-all' or 'inside story' set up for you?

2 From what you have read, would you want to keep reading further to get the author's insights into the restaurant trade?

 Stretch zone

Imagine you are starting your first job some years from now. Write a short text about your first day at work.

Talk about ...

- Would you do a job that was 'paid peanuts', or even work for free, if it was a good opportunity?
- Do you like to read insider stories or 'confidential' stories about working life?
- Are there any jobs it might be inappropriate or even dangerous to write an insider story about?

Controlling the skies for a living!

Can you imagine controlling the air traffic that surrounds a huge airport? The following is a profile of air traffic controller Becky Evans. The writer of this article spent time with Becky, interviewing her and observing her at work. Notice the direct quotations from the interviewee. Swanwick, the location of the National Air Traffic Control Centre, is in the county of Hampshire, England.

> • Look at how texts are structured and presented in order to influence the reader's point of view

Sky high: the air traffic controller

Profile by Leo Benedictus

"Everyone's always very surprised, actually," says Becky Evans. "When they come into the operations rooms they think it's going to be some mad hubbub of craziness." And she is right. Arriving at the National Air Traffic Control
5 Centre at Swanwick, I did indeed think that. But it isn't. Instead, a mood of nonchalant tranquillity fills the vast, white chamber below us, from where almost all of the aircraft over England and Wales are being controlled.

Casually dressed staff chat calmly in front of their
10 computers. When I am allowed in for a peep, one man is even reading a newspaper in his expensive chair. [...] "It's very quiet," says Evans. "It's a very controlled environment, that's the only way I can describe it. We know when aircraft are going to arrive in the sector, and
15 you know what you have to do with them. And then you pass them on to the next guy." It sounds a disarmingly simple way of describing a very complex job.

And though Evans seems a master of it now, she only got into air traffic control, quite literally, by accident. All set
20 to join the army after university, she snapped a ligament in her knee and was rejected on medical grounds. While she was looking around for alternatives, a friend who had already begun training as a controller recommended the air traffic service. "And the more I read about it," she says,
25 "the more I thought, ooh that sounds right up my street."

So in 1998, aged 21, she headed straight for the College of Air Traffic Control in Bournemouth. And after three
45 years of training, having passed her final exams, she was ready to start moving real planes. Was she nervous

30 that first time? "You're probably wanting me to say that it was more of a big moment than it was. But you have been doing this training for such a long time, and during the training you also do periods on the job. So it's not the first time you've spoken to a pilot on the radio."

35 While hundreds of lives depend on Evans doing her job properly, she has always been perfectly calm about it. "Everybody thinks it's a really stressful job," she says. "But I don't find it stressful. It's very rewarding and satisfying when you've done it, and you've been sitting
40 there for an hour and a half and it's all gone really smoothly. There are moments of high pressure, but the training that you do helps you deal with it. It just becomes second nature, almost."

In Evans's case, this pressure usually means having to
45 deal with the busy times when there are around 25 aircraft an hour jostling for her attention. In her patch of sky – the area above the south-west of England and

- Look at how texts are structured and presented in order to influence the reader's point of view
- Understand the meaning and effect of new and unfamiliar words

50 the southernmost half of Wales – this happens most often at around 4 a.m. when many flights from America begin descending towards London. It then peaks again from 10 a.m., when another surge of planes heads off west once more.

The more dramatic types of pressure, of course, are very rare. Evans reels off a list of different systems, each of
55 which is designed to prevent mid-air collisions, and it certainly sounds as if there are enough of them. While other emergencies happen so infrequently that only once, in eight years as an air traffic controller, has she ever had to deal with one. So then, what does happen
60 in an emergency? "If an aircraft says it's got an engine failure or a decompression or something that is not within your control, you just have to deal with it as best you can at the time."

Usually, this means clearing everything out of its way
65 so the plane can land as soon as possible. And so it proved in Evans's own emergency. "There was smoke in the cockpit," she remembers. "A pilot getting airborne from Bristol called me and said 'Pan, pan, pan, pan!' Pan is like a warning. 'Mayday' means big disaster,
70 need to get down immediately, and 'pan' is the next one down. It's not as serious, basically."

So what happened? "There was nothing wrong with his aircraft, but there was smoke in the cockpit, so he said, 'I want to land immediately.' And Brize Norton is just
75 there, which has a huge runway. So he took off from Bristol, went up two or three thousand feet, and then landed at Brize. And he was absolutely fine." She still cannot resist a little smile at the memory of this comically tiny flight.

80 It is interesting to listen to the way Evans tells this story about "him", as if just one man was involved, when in fact "he" was the pilot of a jet full of passengers. It is a reminder that, while other members of her team plan routes and manage traffic flows, her job is fundamentally
85 about talking to people using the coded language of the skies. "Speedbird123 climb flight level 300," for example, would mean "British Airways flight 123, please could you fly up to an altitude of 30,000 feet? Thanks awfully."

Taken from an article in THE GUARDIAN

?

Becky Evans always dreamed of joining the army, but she also has found that she loves her job as an air traffic controller. Do you think people have just one 'dream job', or are there lots of professions which can suit different people?

Glossary

nonchalant calm and casual; showing no anxiety or excitement

tranquillity the state of being calm and quiet

disarmingly overcoming doubts or fears

jostling pushing roughly, typically in a crowd of people

surge sudden or powerful increase

decompression reduction of air pressure

Learning tip
Dropping the phrases 'he said' and 'she said' in reported speech can make writing more dynamic.

Comprehension

A

1 What is the atmosphere in the control room?
2 How does Becky feel about her job?
3 How does she handle the pressure of this responsibility?
4 What does Becky need to do in an emergency?
5 In what way is the interviewer impressed with Becky?

B

1 The writer incorporates some of his interview questions into the profile as though he is directly addressing the reader. (lines 29, 59, 72) What effect does this create?
2 How does the writer insert his own viewpoint into the conversation he has with Becky? Find examples that show judgement or approval.
3 **a** List all the adverbs that end in -*ly* and identify the word stem.
   b Write two or three of your own sentences using some of these adverbs.

C

1 Becky Evans talks about having to stay calm in high-pressure situations. What other jobs can you think of that involve high pressure?
2 Discuss how you would cope with a job like Becky's.

- Examine how a writer's use of language and grammatical features creates effect and meaning
- Apply knowledge of vocabulary, structure and organization of writing in order to influence the reader

Language tip
Adding the suffix -*ly* turns a **verb** or an **adjective** into an **adverb**. These are useful words because they can intensify the language and opinions expressed. For example: 'nice' becomes 'nicely'.

Stretch zone

Start making a note of the different ways that dialogue can be reported in the first, second or third person.

Think of other ways that conversation and communications are usefully incorporated in an account. Use these to compile a handy reference guide for your own writing.

- Write a range of non-fiction texts with confidence, clarity and precision

Writing a 'day-in-the-life-of' profile

It's your turn to be a journalist! You have been commissioned by a magazine to write a profile for their weekly column called *A Day in the Life of* …, in which people discuss their working lives.

- To gather information, you are going to interview someone you know about their job or career. Think of questions that will help you understand the personal motivations and professional skills involved.

- Once you have collected information, select the best material to include in the profile. You can give the person a pseudonym (a made-up name) if you want to. Make sure you include a few direct quotations.

- Swap your profile with a partner's and provide each other with feedback.

Learning tip
Open-ended questions
can prompt an interviewee to give more detailed and interesting answers than 'yes/no' questions. You could ask questions like:

"What made you first think about becoming a …?"

"What do you like/dislike about your job?"

"How did you get started in this industry?"

"Did you think you would be doing this job when you were 14?"

"In what ways are you suited to your job?"

- Examine and discuss a wide range of texts
- Analyze the way an author develops character, setting and plot

Working smarter!

Loosely based on the writer's own childhood, *The Adventures of Tom Sawyer* by American writer Mark Twain is about a boy who grows up on the Mississippi River in the late 1800s.

The story follows Tom's adventures as he learns the ways of the world. In this extract, he is painting, or whitewashing, a fence for his aunt. How does Tom trick his friend into doing the work for him?

Painting the fence

Tom went on whitewashing – paid no attention to the steamboat. Ben stared a moment and then said: "Hi-yi! You're up a stump, ain't you!"

5   No answer. Tom surveyed his last touch with the eye of an artist, then he gave his brush another gentle sweep and surveyed the result, as before. Ben ranged up alongside of him. Tom's mouth watered for the apple
10   that Ben was eating, but he stuck to his work.

Ben said: "Hello, old chap, you got to work, hey?"

Tom wheeled suddenly and said: "Why, it's you, Ben!
15   I warn't noticing."

"Say – I'm going in a-swimming, I am. Don't you wish you could? But of course you'd druther *work* – wouldn't you? Course you would!"

Tom contemplated the boy a bit, and said: "What do you
20   call work?"

"Why, ain't *that* work?"

Tom resumed his whitewashing, and answered carelessly: "Well, maybe it is, and maybe it ain't. All I know is, it suits Tom Sawyer."

A paddle steamer like this one was coming into dock at the opening of the story.

25 "Oh come, now, you don't mean to let on that you *like* it?"

The brush continued to move.

"Like it? Well, I don't see why I oughtn't to like it. Does a boy get a chance to
30 whitewash a fence every day?"

That put the thing in a new light. Ben stopped nibbling his apple. Tom swept his brush daintily back and forth – stepped back to note the effect – added a touch
35 here and there – criticized the effect again – Ben watching every move and getting more and more interested, more and more absorbed. Presently he said:

"Say, Tom, let *me* whitewash a little."

40 Tom considered, was about to consent; but changed his mind: "No-no – I reckon it wouldn't hardly do, Ben. You see, Aunt Polly's awful particular about this fence – right here on the street,
45 you know – but if it was the back fence I wouldn't mind and she wouldn't. Yes, she's awful particular about this fence; it's got to be done very careful; I reckon there ain't one boy in a thousand, maybe two thousand, that can do it the way it's got to be done."

50 "No – is that so? Oh come, now – lemme just try. Only just a little – I'd let *you*, if you was me, Tom."

"Ben, I'd like to … but Aunt Polly – well, Jim wanted to do it, but she wouldn't let him; Sid wanted to do it, and she wouldn't let Sid. Now don't you see how I'm fixed? If you was to tackle
55 this fence and anything was to happen to it –"

"Oh, shucks, I'll be just as careful. Now lemme try. Say – I'll give you the core of my apple."

Glossary

whitewash mixture of lime and water, for whitening walls, ceilings, fence posts, etc.

shucks slang word to express mild disappointment

- Understand the meaning
  and effect of new and
  unfamiliar words

"Well, here – No, Ben, now don't. I'm afeard –"

"I'll give you *all* of it!"

60 Tom gave up the brush with reluctance in his face, but enthusiasm
in his heart. And while the late steamer Big Missouri worked
and sweated in the sun, the retired artist sat on a barrel in the
shade close by, dangled his legs, munched his apple, and planned
the slaughter of more innocents. There was no lack of material;
65 boys happened along every little while; they came to jeer, but
remained to whitewash. Tom had traded the next chance to
Billy Fisher for a kite, in good repair; and when he played out,
Johnny Miller bought in for a dead rat and a string to swing
it with – and so on, and so on, hour after hour. And when the
70 middle of the afternoon came, from being a poor poverty-
stricken boy in the morning, Tom was literally rolling in wealth.
He had besides the things before mentioned, twelve marbles,
a piece of blue bottle-glass to look through, a spool cannon, a
key that wouldn't unlock anything, a fragment of chalk, a glass
75 stopper of a decanter, a tin soldier, a couple of tadpoles, six
fire-crackers, a kitten with only one eye, a brass doorknob, a
dog-collar – but no dog – the handle of a knife, four pieces of
orange-peel, and a dilapidated old window sash.

He had had a nice, good, idle time all the while – plenty of
80 company – and the fence had three coats of whitewash on it!
If he hadn't run out of whitewash he would have bankrupted
every boy in the village.

Tom said to himself that it was not such a hollow world, after
all. He had discovered a great law of human action, without
85 knowing it – namely, that in order to make a man or a boy
covet a thing, it is only necessary to make the thing difficult to
attain. If he had been a great and wise philosopher, like the
writer of this book, he would now have comprehended that
Work consists of whatever a body is *obliged* to do, and that
90 Play consists of whatever a body is not obliged to do. And this
would help him to understand why constructing artificial
flowers or performing on a tread-mill is work, while rolling
ten-pins or climbing Mont Blanc is only amusement. There are
wealthy gentlemen in England who drive four-horse passenger-
95 coaches twenty or thirty miles on a daily line, in the summer,

Glossary

spool cannon slingshot made
out of a cotton-reel
dilapidated falling to pieces,
in disrepair
covet wish to have
something that belongs
to someone else
attain succeed in doing or
getting something

Language tip
Colloquial or 'vernacular'
language is the way people
speak in real life in a
particular community. Writers
often try to capture the
qualities of spoken language.

This includes misspelling,
joining and abbreviating.

- Examine how a writer's use of language and grammatical features creates effect and meaning
- Explain how an author develops character, setting and plot

because the privilege costs them considerable money; but if they were offered wages for the service, that would turn it into work and then they would resign.

100 The boy thought about the substantial change which had taken place in his worldly circumstances, and then wended toward headquarters to report.

From *The Adventures of Tom Sawyer* by MARK TWAIN

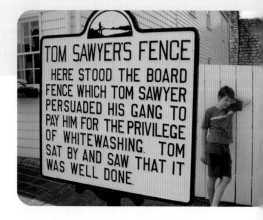

Mark Twain's boyhood home and Tom Sawyer fence in the town of Hannibal, Missouri, USA

Comprehension

1 Why does Tom take his time before saying to Ben, "Why, it's you, Ben! I warn't noticing"? (lines 14–15)

2 What substantial change has taken place in Tom's worldly status by the end of the extract?

3 What does the phrase 'wended toward headquarters' imply about Tom's new sense of himself? (lines 100–101)

1 Can you explain the meaning of the expression "You're up a stump"? (lines 3–4)

2 What is the colloquial form of 'it isn't' which is used several times?

3 What phrases are the words 'druther' and 'lemme' short for?

4 What suffix are the adverbs 'awful' and 'careful' missing?

1 How is the trick Tom Sawyer plays on the other boys an example of exploitation or opportunism? Who are the losers, if any, in his actions?

2 Set up a debate in your classroom to argue the case for and against Tom Sawyer's actions.

Glossary

opportunism using situations unfairly to gain advantage for yourself

Stretch zone

Write an imagined conversation between Tom Sawyer and his Aunt Polly following his fence whitewashing operation. Has she found out how he did it, or does she think he painted it all himself? Consider the language, register and tone each of them would use.

Language tip

Starting a sentence with 'if' is a way of introducing an imaginary past action as a form of the conditional. Pay attention to the use of modal verbs in the following example from the text: 'If he hadn't run out of whitewash he would have bankrupted every boy in the village.'

Children's working conditions in 1832

In 1832, Michael Sadler, an English reformer, led a parliamentary investigation into the working conditions in the textile factories of England, Scotland and Wales. The immediate effect of the report was the passing of the Factory Act of 1833, making it illegal for children under nine years of age to work in textile factories. Children aged between nine and thirteen were not allowed to work more than 48 hours per week.

The following account is from one of many interviews undertaken to compile evidence for the Sadler Committee Report, 1832.

Peter Smart, called in and examined

You say you were locked up night and day? — *Yes.*

Do the children ever attempt to run away? — *Very often.*

Were they pursued and brought back again? — *Yes, the overseer pursued them, and brought them back.*

5   Did you ever attempt to run away? — *Yes, I ran away twice.*

And you were brought back? — *Yes, and I was sent up to the master's loft, and thrashed with a whip for running away.*

Were you bound to this man? — *Yes, for six years.*

By whom were you bound? — *My mother got 15s for the*
10 *six years.*

Do you know whether the children were, in point of fact, compelled to work during the whole time they were engaged? — *Yes, they were.*

By law? — *I cannot say by law, but they were compelled by*
15 *the master. I never saw any law used there but the law of their own hands.*

To what mill did you next go? — *To Mr Webster's, at Battus Den, within eleven miles of Dundee.*

In what situation did you act there? — *I acted as overseer.*

20 At 17 years of age? — *Yes.*

Did you inflict the same punishment that you yourself had experienced? — *I went as an overseer; not as a slave, but as a slave-driver.*

25 What were the hours of labour in that mill? — *My master told me that I had to produce a certain quantity of yarn, the hours were at that time fourteen. I said that I was not able to produce the quantity of yarn that was required. I told him if he took the timepiece out of the mill I would produce that quantity, and after that time I found no difficulty in producing the quantity.*

30 How long have you worked per day in order to produce the quantity your master required? — *I have worked for nineteen hours.*

Was this a water-mill? — *Yes, water and steam, both.*

To what time have you worked? — *I have seen the mill going*
35 *till it was past 12 o'clock on the Saturday night.*

Were the workmen paid by the piece, or by the day? — *No, all had stated wages.*

Did not that almost compel you to use great severity to the hands then under you? — *Yes, I was compelled often to beat*
40 *them, in order to get them to attend to their work, from their being over-wrought.*

Were not the children exceedingly fatigued at that time? — *Yes, exceedingly fatigued.*

Did you find that the children were unable to pursue their
45 labour properly to that extent? — *Yes, they have been brought to that condition, that I have gone and fetched up the doctor to them, to see what was the matter with them, and to know whether they were able to rise or not. We have had great difficulty in getting them up out of bed.*

50 When that was the case, how long have they been in bed, generally speaking? — *Perhaps not above four or five hours in their beds.*

- Read and compare non-fiction texts and discuss their features
- Examine how a writer's use of language and grammatical features creates effect and meaning

Glossary

overseer factory foreman or floor manager

bound having a legal agreement which forces a labourer to work

15s an amount of **fifteen shillings** or 75 pence, less than one pound sterling currency

Dundee on the North Sea is the fourth largest city in Scotland

Language tip
The **passive voice** is useful in reportage and criminal investigation as it enables the interviewer to get a response to their enquiry by focusing on what is being acted upon (the object of the verb) to identify the unknown subject or outcome. So the question is often posed in the passive voice to encourage a response in the **active voice**.

For example:
'Were they pursued and brought back again? — Yes, the overseer pursued them, and brought them back.'
(lines 3–4)

Comprehension

A

1 What is 'the law of their own hands'? (lines 15–16)
2 What is Peter's definition of an overseer's role?
3 What is the significance of the timepiece in Peter's account?
4 What does it mean to be paid by the piece instead of by the day?
5 Why do you think Peter's mother allowed her son to be 'bound'?

B

1 Read again the following lines from the report and rewrite them in contemporary language:
   a "By whom were you bound?" (line 9)
   b "To what mill did you next go?" (line 17)
   c "In what situation did you act there?" (line 19)
   d "Were not the children exceedingly fatigued at that time?" (line 42)

C

1 What things would make you question the values and ethics of an industry or workplace today?
2 Can you think of any industries today which you would reform if you could?
3 What do you think the motivations and goals of workplace reform should be? Discuss the issues with your class or group.

- Read and compare non-fiction texts and discuss their features
- Examine how a writer's use of language and grammatical features creates effect and meaning

?

How should people be treated to make sure that they don't have to choose between being a slave or a slave driver in the workplace?

Boys working in a spinning mill, 1910

Your turn to present

In some countries, economic circumstances mean that children are forced to work. What effects do you think this has on the children?

There are many organizations which work to protect children. Research one such organization and find out what it has achieved.

- Find out about the aims of the organization and when and how it was started.
- Find out how the organization has helped children and give examples of children whose lives have been improved as a result.
- Present your research to your group in a five-minute presentation.

Allow enough time after your presentations to compare and contrast the different organizations you have chosen. Do they all take a similar approach in combating child labour, or are there differences? What do you think is the most effective approach?

- Participate fully in discussions
- Discuss ideas with others, questioning and evaluating opposing views
- Carry out comprehensive research on a range of topics
- Use verbal and non-verbal techniques when presenting information to aid understanding

Talk about ...

- What do you know about child labour laws in your country?
- If children are allowed to work, what is being done to limit the hours they work so that their health doesn't suffer and they can attend school?

Marching against child labour in Tacloban, the Philippines

The weather

How does the weather affect our way of life?

'To meet an old friend in a distant country is like thc delight of rain after a long drought.'

Chinese Proverb

Talk about ...

- Why is the weather so important?
- What do you like and dislike about the weather where you live?
- What can we do to protect ourselves from the harmful effects of extreme weather?

The seasonal weather patterns of countries differ across the globe and have many different effects on the people living there. For example, in parts of Asia people suffer sweltering, intense heat and long for the monsoon rains to arrive. The proverb which opens this unit reflects the relief people feel once the rains finally arrive.

- Look at how texts are structured and presented in order to influence the reader's point of view

Living in sub-zero temperatures

Louisa Waugh spent a year working as an English teacher in a remote village in the Altai mountains in the far north-west of Mongolia, close to the border with Siberia in Russia. She sent monthly newsletters to a British journal. Here is an excerpt from one describing a typical winter morning.

A frozen world

I wake up and my world has frozen. Everything, and I mean everything – my water, tomato paste, soap – is encased in thick, milky ice. I light a candle, stand up in my sleeping bag and pull on another layer of
5 clothing. Shivering, I take a knife to the water bucket and hack at the ice until bubbles rise to the surface. Lighting my small stove is difficult because the wood, which was damp, is now frozen. By the
10 time my smoky fire is finally crackling and heating the water and ice in the kettle, the outside temperature has risen to –25°C. I've never been so cold in my life. I know the mountains surrounding my village
15 will be covered in fresh snow but I can't see anything because my window is coated with thick ice. On this dark, freezing winter morning, venturing to the communal outside toilet is quite an endurance test.
20 But, after two cups of steaming black coffee I am wrapped up and off to work, just as the sky is gradually brightening.

My school is a ten-minute walk alongside the Hovd river which flows through the
25 village. The river has now frozen so solid that horses are being ridden and cars driven over it. Everything but my eyes is concealed from the freezing air and my gloved fingers are pushed down into my pockets.

30 "Off to work, Louisa?" calls my neighbour, Sansar-Huu. "Don't worry, it's quite warm today – just wait till it gets really cold!"

- Look at how texts are structured and presented in order to influence the reader's point of view

Our school has no electricity or running water, but each small classroom is heated by a wood-burning stove. This morning we all wear our coats during lessons. Wind-burned children 35 from herders' settlements outside the village board at the school, twelve to a dormitory. Their parents pay the fees in meat and wood. At break we jostle to be near the staff-room stove and my colleagues pull their fur hats back on.

"You sit by the fire, Louisa – you must be freezing," offers 40 Gansukh, my fellow English teacher.

After our classes, Gansukh and I cross the street to the post office, which is crowded, as the weekly post has arrived. Clutching two letters, I walk home with Gansukh and a couple of our students, passing herders trading camel, sheep, goat and 45 wolf skins. We stop *en route* for bowls of tea at a friend's house.

At home, I need more water. I lift the creaking lid of the well opposite our yard, but the water is frozen so hard that I can hear the rocks I fling down the shaft ricochet off the ice. Taking the axe, I set out for the nearby river to make my own well.

50 That afternoon it snows heavily as Sansar-Huu and I saw logs in the yard. "How long will it be this cold?" I ask him as I stand panting, my face flushed and numb. "Oh, it gets as low as –48°C here," he tells me, grinning. "But we need this snowy winter. Even by October it's really too cold to live in a felt *ger*

Glossary

communal shared by several people

endurance ability to put up with difficulty or pain for a long period

concealed hidden, covered

herder someone who looks after a herd of animals

settlement small number of people or houses established in a new area

ricochet bounce off a surface, rebound

livestock farm animals

A Mongolian yurt

55 here – so the herders in the mountains move up into their winter log cabins. Their livestock live on hay and the herders melt snow for all their water. They slaughter sheep for food at the start of winter, when the animals are still fat, and the ice preserves the meat till the end of spring."

60 "So, if the snow comes late, like it did this year, what then?" I ask.

"That's when the steppe gets overgrazed, which means spring will be very tough. Remember those trucks loaded up with ice driving way into the mountains?" I nod. "The ice was for herders
65 who didn't have enough snow and weren't near the rivers …"

Sansar-Huu pauses to wave and call greetings to a local who trots past, his horse crusted in frozen sweat. I look around me at the snowscape – silent mountains on all four sides, pack camels weighed down with flour and hay, children skating on
70 the river – and the deep snow … I pick up the axe and raise it to my shoulder just as Sansar-Huu turns back to me. "The herders are fine now," he says. "The snow is here for the winter."

From 'Letters from Tsengel, Mongolia' by Louisa Waugh

Talk about …

- Does the climate you live in bring daily challenges?
- Imagine you are going to live in a country with the opposite weather to the country you live in now. What challenges do you think this might bring?
- What is the most extreme climate you have ever experienced?

Word origins

ger (or 'yurt') (n), Mongolian house made of leather and felt stretched over a wooden framework. *Ger* in Mongolian means 'home'.

the steppe (n), expanse of treeless grassland in Mongolia and Russia. From German *Steppe* or French *steppe*, meaning 'flat, grassy plain'.

- Adapt writing style and register for intended audience and purpose
- Write a range of non-fiction texts
- Proofread and edit writing

Comprehension

 A

1 Describe some difficulties of the writer's morning routine.
2 What have you learned about the herders' way of life?
3 Why did trucks take ice up to the herders?
4 How will the axe help the writer to make her own well?

 B

1 Choose the right preposition to go with the verb. Read through the extract to find the missing prepositions:

   a to wake _____
   b to wrap _____
   c to drive _____
   d to conceal _____
   e to sit _____
   f to look _____

2 Analyze the use of dashes in this extract. Find three examples in the text and explain how the author has chosen to use them.

 C

1 How effective is this text in conveying to the reader what the experience is like living in such an extremely cold and isolated place?
2 Why is living in an extreme climate or remote settlement more likely to bring people together? Think of other examples of supportive communities that you know of and compare them with the community described in the extract.

> **Language tip**
> The **dash** is a useful punctuation mark for inserting additional information or examples to a sentence.
>
> - A single dash at the end of the sentence can be followed by a whole phrase, or just one word, as in the example: 'Everyone needs them – friends.'
>
> - Two dashes (also known as parenthetical dashes) can be used in the middle of a sentence, as in the example: 'You are the friend – the only friend – who can help me.'

A different weather experience!

Write your own newsletter or blog post about the experience of living somewhere that has an extreme or unusual climate. It can be a real or imagined experience.

- What challenges did you have to face, and how did you manage them?
- Include plenty of interesting details and descriptions, as well as information about the accommodation provided, the land and environment, including any local wildlife, and the customary habits of the people you met.
- Swap your writing with a partner and offer constructive feedback on each other's work.

> **Learning tip**
> A newsletter (like a blog post) is different from a private letter or message, as it is addressed to a more general reader rather than one person.

Is the weather alive?

In the very short poem 'Fog', the American poet Carl Sandburg uses zoomorphism to talk about the fog through an extended metaphor. This means that he describes the fog as a living creature.

Fog

The fog comes
On little cat feet

It sits looking
Over harbor and city
5 On silent haunches
And then moves on.

CARL SANDBURG

Write your own weather poem

Now it's your turn! Write your own poem using an extended metaphor to compare an aspect of the weather with some other kind of living being such as a plant, animal or human being.

- Come up with your own imaginative comparison using any type of weather, paired with any type of living being you can think of.

- Make a list of all the useful points of comparison and include appropriate descriptive details to help you write your poem. If it helps to visualize your 'weather being', draw an accompanying illustration.

- Look at a variety of texts and evaluate how writers develop ideas and themes in their writing
- Consider how poets play with themes and conventions in a range of poetic forms
- Write a range of different fiction genres and poetry
- Use literary and rhetorical devices to enhance the impact of writing

Language tip
An **extended metaphor** is a metaphor that is developed in great detail to show how something is similar to something else in lots of ways.

Zoomorphism means giving something the characteristics of an animal. It can be compared to the concept of **anthropomorphism**, which means giving something non-human the characteristics of a person.

Stretch zone

Poems about our experience of the natural world can communicate with other human beings across time and space.

Find other examples of short poetry or prose that interest you. Share them with the rest of the class.

Amazing lights

The following account of witnessing the northern lights was written in Bohemia in 1570. Bohemia is in Central Europe, and is now part of the Czech Republic. When this account was written, people didn't understand that auroras (polar lights) were caused by magnetic storms in the Earth's upper atmosphere.

What does this account reveal about the fears and beliefs of those who observed the astonishing effects?

- Read literature from different historical periods
- Distinguish between statements of fact and of opinion in texts to identify the viewpoint of the writer

An uncommon omen

An uncommon omen was observed among the clouds over Bohemia on the 12th January, 1570. It lasted four hours. First, a black cloud like a great mountain appeared where several stars had been shining. Above the cloud there was a bright
5   strip of light as of burning sulphur and in the shape of a ship. From this arose many burning torches, almost like candles, and between these, two great pillars, one to the east and one to the north. Fire coursed down the pillars like drops of blood, and the town was illuminated as if it were on fire. The watchmen
10 sounded the alarm and woke the inhabitants so they could witness this miraculous sign from God. All were dismayed and said that never within the memory of man had they seen or heard tell of such a sinister sight.

A view of the aurora borealis (also called the northern lights)

Comprehension

1 What does this account reveal about the knowledge and belief system of the sixteenth-century inhabitants of Bohemia?

2 List the key observations and compare them with what you know of the physical and atmospheric effects that create auroras.

3 How do the imagery and the events described in this text reflect the times they were written in?

1 Which words in the text tell you the inhabitants were unhappy?

2 List all the phrases in the text that show the speaker witnessed something unusual and important.

1 How is the worldview of the writer different to how we view the world today?

2 From the point of view of the present times, what is useful about this historical account?

Dangerous weather

These opening scenes from William Shakespeare's play *The Tempest* are set on an island in the Mediterranean Sea. The play was written around 1610–1611, at a time when Europeans were starting to set sail on voyages of discovery to other parts of the world, resulting in many shipwrecks and deaths at sea, as well as extraordinary tales of survival.

In this extract, we witness an exchange between the Boatswain (pronounced 'bòsun') and Antonio, the Duke of Milan, representing the royal party who are ordered below deck due to the dangerous and stormy conditions. Later in Scene 2, from the shore, we are introduced to Prospero and Miranda, the former Duke of Milan and his daughter. They are castaways on the island from a previous shipwreck.

- Examine and discuss a wide range of texts, including classic texts
- Examine how texts mirror events of the time and place they were written
- Read literature from different historical periods

The Tempest

Act I, Scene 1

On a ship at sea: a tempestuous noise of thunder and lightning heard. Enter a Master and a Boatswain.

Master	Boatswain!
Boatswain	Here, master: what cheer?
5 **Master**	Good, speak to the mariners: fall to't, yarely, or we run ourselves aground: bestir, bestir.

He exits. The crew enter.

Boatswain   Heigh, my hearts! cheerly, cheerly, my hearts! yare, yare! Take in the topsail. Tend to the master's whistle.
10   Blow, till thou burst thy wind, if room enough!

Enter Alonso, Sebastian, Antonio, Gonzalo, and others.

Alonso   Good boatswain, have care. Where's the master? Play the men.

Boatswain   I pray now, keep below.

15 **Antonio**   Where is the master, boatswain?

Boatswain   Do you not hear him? You mar our labour: keep your cabins: you do assist the storm.

Gonzalo   Nay, good, be patient.

Boatswain   When the sea is. Hence! What cares these roarers for
20   the name of king? To cabin: silence! trouble us not.

Gonzalo   Good, yet remember whom thou hast aboard.

Learning tip
Shakespeare's language can be a challenge to understand today. Try reading an annotated edition that includes a glossary of tricky words. Even better, watch a performance at the theatre, cinema or online. Remember that you don't need to understand every single word or phrase. Understanding the language does get easier, so make sure you persevere!

- Identify evidence in a text about the environment, culture and social situation
- Examine and discuss a wide range of texts, including classic texts
- Read literature from different historical periods

Boatswain None that I more love than myself. You are a counsellor; if you can command these elements to silence, and work the peace of the present, we will
25 not hand a rope more; use your authority: if you cannot, give thanks you have lived so long, and make yourself ready in your cabin for the mischance of the hour, if it so hap. Cheerly, good hearts! Out of our way, I say.

30 *He exits.* [...] *Re-enter Boatswain.*

Boatswain Down with the topmast! yare! lower, lower! Bring her to try with main-course.

A cry within.

A plague upon this howling! they are louder than
35 the weather or our office.

Re-enter Sebastian, Antonio, and Gonzalo.

Yet again! what do you here? Shall we give o'er and drown? Have you a mind to sink?

A confused noise within: "Mercy on us!" – "We split, we split!"
40 – "Farewell, my wife and children!" – "Farewell, brother!"
– "We split, we split, we split!"

Antonio Let's all sink with the king.

Sebastian Let's take leave of him.

Antonio and Sebastian exit.

45 **Gonzalo** Now would I give a thousand furlongs of sea for an acre of barren ground, long heath, brown furze, any thing. The wills above be done! but I would fain die a dry death.

He exits.

Act I, Scene 2

50 *The island. Enter Prospero and Miranda.*

Miranda The sky, it seems, would pour down stinking pitch, But that the sea, mounting to the welkin's cheek, Dashes the fire out. O, I have suffered With those that I saw suffer: a brave vessel,
55 Who had, no doubt, some noble creatures in her, Dash'd all to pieces. O, the cry did knock Against my very heart. Poor souls, they perish'd.

From *The Tempest* by WILLIAM SHAKESPEARE

Glossary

boatswain a ship's officer in charge of rigging, boats and anchors (pronounced 'bow sun')

yarely quickly

hearts hearties, good fellows

furlong measure of distance equal to about 220 yards – from the Old English *furlang* meaning 'furrow long', the length of a furrow in a field

fain pleased or willing to

welkin's sky's

Miranda watches the ship in peril

- Identify evidence in a text about the environment, culture and social situation
- Examine how writers use a variety of language and grammatical features to create different effects and meaning
- Read literature from different historical periods
- Discuss the meaning and effect of new and unfamiliar words

Comprehension

1 Why does the Boatswain insist that the passengers of the ship 'keep below'? (line 14) What is he concerned about?

2 What are the elements the Boatswain is referring to when he says 'if you can command these elements to silence'? (lines 23–24)

3 In line 34, who or what is he referring to as 'howling'?

1 In your own words, explain the meaning of the following words and phrases in context:

   a 'you do assist the storm' (line 17)

   b 'these roarers' (line 19)

   c 'barren ground' (line 46)

   d 'die a dry death' (line 48)

   e 'a brave vessel' (line 54)

2 What does the imagery in Miranda's speech reveal about what she observed from the shore?

1 There is some tension between the different characters on board the ship. What does this show about the social hierarchy on board, and are there any consequences from it?

2 What do you think the human cost of the storm is? Think about how the storm is presented in the extract, and how the idea of a storm or a 'tempest' might work as an extended metaphor.

Stage the storm

In small groups, make notes on how you would stage the scenes above. How would you make it clear that the action is happening on a boat at sea and on an island? How should the actors behave and use their bodies? What about the tone of voice they use? Then divide up the roles and practise performing the scenes, taking into account the staging notes you made before.

Perform to another group and ask them for feedback.

Language tip
Shakespeare is famous for his use of **word play** through **joking puns** and **extended metaphor**. For example, a speech from the play *As You Like It* begins:

'All the world's a stage,
And all the men and women merely players …'

The meaning of this extended metaphor is that we all play many different parts in our lifetime, and we are all performing as ourselves in daily life.

A storm is coming

The following extract comes from a novel set in Turkey. Mehmet has moved with his family from the country to the city of Ankara in search of a better life. But the family have to live in a shanty town outside the city. Mehmet makes a friend called Muhlis, and they are occasionally employed by Zekiye Hanim to work in her garden. They go to her house by cart pulled by Yildiz, Muhlis's horse. On this occasion, the weather has been getting increasingly hot and a storm is threatening.

Mehmet lived in a shanty town like this one.

The storm

It was hotter still. Mehmet's mother had nailed sheets over most of the empty windows but it was impossible to keep the house cool. By day they were plagued with flies. They settled on your food as you raised the spoon to your mouth and they
5   crawled along your eyelids and round your nose. With the coming of darkness, the mosquitoes rose up in great, humming clouds. Even when you thought you had covered yourself completely with a sheet, the high whine of yet another disturbed your sleep. The children scratched and scratched until they
10 bled. Tonight it was extra bad. The older people said that there was a storm coming: flies always came indoors before a storm. Once Mehmet awoke and he sat with his grandfather and they watched the lightning forking in the distance, but no rain fell. In the morning he was to go to Zekiye Hanim's house, so

15 Mehmet was glad to get up early. He sharpened the scythe, and then hurried out on hearing the clink of Yildiz's hooves. It was oppressively hot. A sudden flurry blew the dust up into their faces. The wind was warm and the grit grated between their teeth. They urged Yildiz on, eager to reach
20 the cooling green of the walled garden.

They set to work, Mehmet scything the grass and Muhlis weeding between the rose bushes. It was too hot to talk and the garden was quieter than they had ever known it. Not a leaf stirred. The cut grass
25 shrivelled as soon as it fell. Zekiye Hanim, who liked to talk and help a little, sat on the balcony and fanned herself and looked out to the distant mountains. She said that a storm must come. At lunch-time they knocked on the door and fetched
30 their tray of bread, olives and fruit and searched for the shade. Today the shadows were warm. They soaked their heads and shirts with water from the hose, trying to refresh themselves, but their clothes felt heavy and chill instead. After
35 lunch they raked the grass into a pile and then they began sweeping and washing the paths and steps. Suddenly Zekiye Hanim banged on the window and shook her head, as if she did not want them to continue working. She pointed repeatedly to something in the distance and when they did not understand
40 she came back on to the balcony.

Scythes leaning up against a woodshed

"Your work will be wasted. Look over there: don't you see the storm coming?"

"I don't see any clouds," said Mehmet, "really I don't. Let us tidy up for you."

45 "Some storms come without clouds. If you know the signs you can tell. Look!"

"I can't see anything," said Mehmet. "It looks to me like the sun is shining on the mountains."

"Look more carefully."

50 "I can see a brightness and the mountains have a dark line around them." Then he shivered: a sharp, twirling wind went

Glossary

scythe tool with a long curved blade for cutting grass or corn

oppressive weather that is hot and humid

flurry sudden whirling gust, also a short burst of activity

twirling turning around in a circle

cone object that is circular at one end and narrows to a point

over the garden and up the street. They heard windows bang and the scratch of dry papers blown along the base of the wall. He shivered again. [...]

55 "Now," insisted Zekiye Hanim, "look again. I've known it was coming for a long time, though I hoped that it would not."

"Do you see that?" called Muhlis. The light behind the mountains – a strange greenish-yellow light – became brighter and there, far beyond the other side of the great city were three cones of
60 darkness, which looked as though a giant hand had scribbled them in the sky. As they watched, the cones grew in size.

Learning tip
As you read through this text, pay attention to the use of **reported speech** and the **different tenses**. Think about how the variety enriches the description of the experience presented in the text.

"Is it smoke?" Mehmet wondered if something very big was burning.

"No, it's the wind ..."

65 "But you can't see the wind ..."

"It's the dirt and dust caught up in the wind. In about half an hour it will be here. It'll be a very strong wind."

?

How does poor housing make the effects of extreme weather worse? Think of examples that you know of in your home town or country.

"Strong enough to blow things down?" Mehmet thought anxiously of his family in that half-finished building. Another
70 gust rustled the leaves in the garden.

"It'll be strong enough to blow a few roofs off. Now, do you still want to help me?"

They nodded. "Then take your shoes off and come indoors quickly and help me fasten down all the
75 shutters and windows before that wind reaches us." They dropped their tools hastily and entered the house.

The sky was darkening rapidly and it was not with the coming of evening. The yellow light was deepening
80 and the brightness fading. They quickly started untying the cushions from the white chairs, and began to pack away the furniture on the balcony. Another strong gust thrust against the balcony doors as they tried to shut them. From somewhere up the
85 street they heard glass breaking. Outside, the roses glowed very clearly in the lightless garden.

- Examine how a writer's use of language and grammatical features creates effects and meanings
- Find evidence in a text about the environment, culture and social situation

"You had better get that grass into the sacks before the wind really comes," she reminded them and they ran barefoot into the garden. They saw papers swept high up and spinning around
90 in the air, high above the trees. The heap of grass lifted and began to fan upwards. Muhlis leapt forward with his arms outstretched to try and save it. He seemed to stumble. He did not cry out. They heard a gasping sound as though the wind had torn his words from him. Then he curled up on the ground
95 with his hands around his foot. He had trodden heavily on to the curved blade of the scythe that Mehmet had hastily flung down amongst the grass cuttings.

From *Against the Storm* by Gaye Hiçyilmaz

Comprehension

1 What signs are there of the approaching storm?
2 What does Mehmet mean by describing his family's house as a 'half-finished building'?
3 What do you think the 'three cones of darkness' represent? (lines 59–60)
4 What mistake did Mehmet make that caused his friend a serious injury?

1 Explain these phrases and expressions:
   a 'plagued with flies' (line 3)
   b 'great humming clouds' (lines 6–7)
   c 'a sudden flurry' (line 17)
   d 'a sharp, twirling wind' (line 51)
2 How does the writer create a sense of imminent threat and danger?

1 Storms are often used as a metaphor or backdrop to other types of breakdowns or catastrophes. What other works of art, film or literature can you think of that have used the metaphor of the storm to represent different types of human conflict?

Stretch zone

Imagine you are a director dramatizing this scene for the theatre. How would you build tension and atmosphere on stage using lighting and sound effects? What instructions about delivering their lines (for example, regarding tone and expression) would you give to the actors playing Mehmet, Muhlis and Zekiye?

6 Being free

What does it mean to be free?

> 'For to be free is not merely to cast off one's chains, but to live in a way that respects and enhances the freedom of others.'
>
> NELSON MANDELA

Talk about ...

- Why is freedom so difficult to define?
- What kind of choices do we have in today's world?
- What does freedom mean to you in your life?

The first article of the United Nations Declaration of Human Rights (1948) states 'We are all born free and equal. We all have our own thoughts and ideas. We should all be treated in the same way.' This human right is a great aspiration, but not everyone would agree that it is universal or respected by all members of the global community.

As you read through the texts in this unit, think about the historical and contemporary conditions of restriction and slavery, and how you personally make the most of your freedoms.

- Consider how poets play with different themes and conventions

Is there such a thing as a free country?

The English poet Adrian Mitchell wrote about his desire for peace and social equality; both are necessary to create freedom. In the following poem, he writes about the idea of a free country. Do you think such a country exists?

Glossary

ragamuffin person dressed in scruffy clothes

Secret Country

There is no money
So there's no crime
There are no watches
Cos there's no time
5 It's a good country
It's a secret country
And it's your country and mine

If you need something
You make it there
10 And we have plenty
For we all share
It's a kind country
It's a secret country
And it's your country and mine

15 There are no cages
There is no zoo
But the free creatures
Come and walk with you
It's a strange country
20 It's a secret country
And it's your country and mine

There are no prisons
There are no poor
There are no weapons
25 There is no war
It's a safe country
It's a secret country
And it's your country and mine

And in that country
30 Grows a great tree
And it's called Freedom
And its fruit is free
In that blue country
In that warm country

35 In that loving country
In that ragamuffin country
In that secret country
Which is your country and mine

Adrian Mitchell

Comprehension

B 🧍

1 What is the significance of the one proper noun in the poem?

2 Choose one stanza from this poem and explain the imagery and associations.

3 Discuss how the poet uses repetition, referring to specific examples from the poem.

4 What effect does the regular rhyme scheme of the poem create for the reader?

5 Why does the poet use the description 'ragamuffin country' in line 36?

6 Why does the poet call it a 'secret' country in lines 6, 13, 20, 27 and 37?

C 👥

1 Do you think the poet believes a country like this could exist? Do you believe it could? Explain why or why not to your partner or group.

> **Language tip**
> A **proper noun** is always capitalized to refer to the name of a particular person, place or thing. Sometimes a concept, philosophical term or abstract principle is also capitalized for emphasis: for example, 'I am telling you the Truth'.

> **?**
> In English, we sometimes use the simile 'to feel free as a bird'. Do you think animals experience freedom the same way as humans do?

Finding a way out

The following text is an extract from a short story called 'If Only Papa Hadn't Danced' by Patricia McCormick. It is a story told from the viewpoint of a young girl and is set in a country which has long been ruled by 'the Old Man', an unjust ruler who committed many human rights abuses.

In this story, the girl's father, her 'Papa', danced and celebrated with other people when the Old Man was beaten in elections. But when the results of the free and fair elections were overturned, it was no longer safe for the family to live in the country. After walking for two days, the family finally reaches the river on the border.

A dangerous border crossing

Mama knelt in the shallows and splashed water on her face. But as I knelt down next to her, I saw that she was trying to cover her tears.

"*This* is our homeland," she said. "No one wants us over
5   there." She gestured to the tawny hills across the river.

It was then that I saw the long metal fence which uncoiled, like a snake, all along the riverbank on the other side. The fence was tall and crowned with rings of wire: wire with teeth that could slice the clothes from your back, the skin
10   from your bones. In the distance I saw a man in an orange jumpsuit patching a hole at the bottom of the fence – a spot where some lucky person must have slipped through the night before. His tools were at his feet, a pistol in his belt.

Papa came over and said I was needed. There was a sign,
15   that he needed me to read: *Beware of crocodiles*.

That night, we hid in the bushes until the sky was black. We would wade across at midnight, when the man in the orange jumpsuit had gone home. [...] When it was time to go, I walked straight towards the river, knowing my nerve
20   would fail if I faltered for even a moment. But Papa stopped me at the water's edge.

"Wait here," he said. And then he scooped Mama up into his arms and waded silently into the darkness.

It seemed a lifetime until he returned. He didn't say a word,

- Compare and contrast a wide range of fiction and non-fiction texts on the same theme
- Look at how texts are structured and presented in order to influence the reader's point of view

Language tip

The phrase 'if only' is used to express a strong wish that things could be different. It means the same as 'I wish' but is stronger. We use it to talk about past, present and future possibilities. In grammatical terms, this is a form of **the conditional**.

A typical sentence using 'if only' is structured in this way:

'If only' + *past verb form* (+ *wish in the conditional tense*)

For example: 'If only I hadn't lost her phone number.' (Implied wish: 'I could ring her'.)

Stretch zone

Look up the different forms of the conditional, and learn how to recognize them.

- Compare and contrast a wide range of fiction and non-fiction texts on the same theme
- Look at how texts are structured and presented in order to influence the reader's point of view

25 just lifted me up onto his shoulders and strode into the water. Every stick I saw was a crocodile. Under every rock, every ripple in the water was a pair of ferocious jaws. When we reached the other side, I leapt from his shoulders and kissed the sand.

30 Once more Papa stepped into the river – this time to fetch our suitcase. Surely our luck wouldn't hold again. [...] Finally Papa emerged from the darkness with all our worldly possessions balanced on his head.

Then we got down on our hands and knees and crawled along
35 the base of the fence, like scorpions looking for a place to dig. But the sand was unyielding and the fence invincible. Everywhere our fingers scrabbled for a weakness, someone – the man in the orange jumpsuit, most likely – had mended it with links of chain held tight with wire.

40 The sky overhead had begun to brighten and the horizon was edged with pink. Soon it would be light and we'd be trapped between the waking crocodiles and the man with the gun in his belt.

We came to a spot in the fence where a thorn bush grew on
45 the other side. Papa said we would have to dig here: no time to keep looking. Perhaps the roots of the bush had loosened the sand, he said. If not, at least we could hide behind the bush, if only for a while.

And so all three of us dug – Mama in the middle and Papa and
50 I on either side – our hands clawing furiously at the earth. I'd only made a few inches of progress when the sky turned red. It would be dawn in less than an hour. [...] Soon I'd dug a hole barely big enough for a man's foot. I lifted my head to call out to Papa to come and see my work – and saw the man in the
55 orange jumpsuit striding towards us. Mama wailed piteously, then plucked at her hem where she'd hidden the tiny bit of money we had. She knelt in the sand, her arms outstretched, our few coins in her upturned palms. But the man shook his head. He placed his hand on the belt that held his gun.

60 "Take me," Papa begged him. "Spare the woman and the girl."

Again the man shook his head. Then he reached into his pocket and took out a giant cutting tool. With one mighty snap he

Glossary

tawny brownish-yellow
unyielding not giving away to pressure
invincible not able to be defeated
piteously deserving of pity
safe house place where those who are running away from danger can seek refuge

- Compare and contrast a wide range of fiction and non-fiction texts on the same theme
- Look at how texts are structured and presented in order to influence the reader's point of view

65 severed the links where the fence had been patched. He yanked on the fence so hard it cried out in protest, and peeled it back as if it were made of cloth.

"Hurry," he said. "Once the light comes, I will have to go back to patrolling." We didn't fully comprehend what he was saying, but we didn't wait.

"You go first," Papa said to me. "I want you to be the first 70 in our family to taste freedom." I scrambled through the fence, stood next to the man in the orange jumpsuit and looked back at our homeland as the sun began to turn its fields to gold.

"You will miss it for a long time," the man said to me. [...] "Yes," 75 he said. "I outran the Old Man long ago." Mama crawled through and kissed the man's boots. He simply helped her to her feet.

"Quickly now," he said, once Papa had made it through.

"Walk, as fast as you can, until you see a house with white 80 flowers out front. [...] They will feed you and hide you until night. Then they will send you to the next safe house, which will send you to the next, and the next – until finally you are in the city and can be swallowed up by all the people there."

"How do we know we can trust these people?" Mama asked.

85 "They are our countrymen," he said. "You will find many of us here. Now go!"

We did as he instructed, and found the house with the white flowers just as the morning sun broke through the clouds. A woman there brought us inside, gave us water and meat and 90 led us to mats where we could rest. [...]

I awoke sometime later and saw that Papa's mat was empty. I stood and wandered outside. The sun was setting, so all I could see was his silhouette against the deepening sky. He raised his arms to the heavens and started to hum. And then 95 I saw Papa dance.

From *If Only Papa Hadn't Danced* by PATRICIA McCORMICK

- Use literary and rhetorical devices to develop writing skills
- Write using a variety of structures for different purposes

Comprehension

1 Why did Papa cross the river more than once?

2 What did the family think was going to happen when the man patrolling the fence approached them?

3 Why did Mama offer the man in the orange jumpsuit the little bit of money they had?

1 Explain how the following similes and images help to create the dramatic atmosphere of the story:

   a 'uncoiled, like a snake' (lines 6–7)

   b 'wire with teeth' (lines 8–9)

   c 'like scorpions looking for a place to dig' (line 35)

2 How significant are the following reference points and images in this story and what effect do they have?

   a crocodiles

   b the Old Man

   c white flowers

3 Reread lines 6–13. How does the writer use a variety of sentence structures for different effects?

1 The story is told from the perspective of the young girl. In what ways does this help to create empathy for the difficult choices the family has to make?

2 Do you think the family are now truly free? Explain your answer.

Stretch zone

Storyboard this extract from the text for a film or graphic novel. Write the dialogue, and document the key features of the characters, scene and setting.

Writing an 'If only …' narrative

Think of a story title starting with 'If only …' and write your own hypothetical narrative.

- Make the most of the opening sentence and/or title to your story, before going into the compelling details and backstory.

- Give lots of detail about the consequences and circumstances of the situation you are describing.

- Think of a way to end your narrative with a positive outcome.

Share your narrative with your partner or group and offer each other feedback.

Word origins

hypothetical (adj), from the ancient Greek *hupothesis*, meaning 'foundation', which comes from *hupo* meaning 'under' and *thesis* meaning 'placing'. It describes an idea that has not yet been proved to be true or correct.

Related words:
- hypothesis
- hypothesize

Slave and master

The opening scenes of William Shakespeare's *The Tempest* were studied in Unit 5. The passengers who were on the ship are now marooned on the island due to the storm caused by Prospero, the master of the island, who lives there alone with his daughter, Miranda, and his slave, Caliban.

Caliban is a native of the island who helped Prospero survive when he first arrived there. Prospero had been cast out of his home by his brother. Prospero rewarded Caliban by making the latter his slave, and now the two hate each other.

- Read literature from different historical periods
- Discuss unfamiliar vocabulary
- Read playscripts with feeling

A thing most brutish

Act I, Scene 2

Miranda	Abhorred slave,
	Which any print of goodness wilt not take,
	Being capable of all ill! I pitied thee,
	Took pains to make thee speak, taught thee each hour
5	One thing or other. When thou didst not, savage,
	Know thine own meaning, but wouldst gabble like
	A thing most brutish, I endow'd thy purposes
	With words that made them known. But thy vile race—
	Though thou didst learn—had that in't which good natures
10	Could not abide to be with; therefore wast thou
	Deservedly confin'd into this rock,
	Who hadst deserv'd more than a prison.
Caliban	You taught me language; and my profit on't
15	Is I know how to curse. The red plague rid you
	For learning me your language!
Prospero	Hag-seed, hence!
	Fetch us in fuel, and be quick, thou'rt best,
	To answer other business—shrug'st thou, malice?
20	If thou neglect'st, or dost unwillingly
	What I command, I'll rack thee with old cramps,
	Fill all thy bones with aches, make thee roar,
	That beasts shall tremble at thy din.
Caliban	No, pray thee.
25	[*Aside*] I must obey.

Caliban in a modern performance of *The Tempest*

Glossary

marooned trapped on an island, unable to escape

Hag-seed son of an old, wrinkled woman

malice wanting to wish someone harm

colonist someone who settles in a colony or county

Talk about ...

What comparisons can we make between Act I, Scene 2 and the colonization of New World countries and how the native populations were treated by the colonists?

Another side to Caliban

In the following scene, Caliban has been scheming with Stephano, a butler who was on the ship, to kill Prospero. They hear strange noises which scare Stephano and this prompts Caliban to talk about his love of the island.

- Read literature from different historical periods
- Discuss unfamiliar vocabulary
- Read playscripts with feeling
- Rewrite a text for a particular audience

Caliban's dreams

Act III, Scene 2

Caliban	Art thou afeard?
Stephano	No, monster, not I.
Caliban	Be not afeard, the isle is full of noises,
	Sounds, and sweet airs, that give delight and hurt not.
5	Sometimes a thousand twangling instruments
	Will hum about mine ears; and sometime voices
	That if I then had wak'd after long sleep,
	Will make me sleep again, and then in dreaming
	The clouds methought would open and show riches
10	Ready to drop upon me that, when I wak'd,
	I cried to dream again.

From *The Tempest* by WILLIAM SHAKESPEARE

Glossary

butler senior servant in a house

Comprehension

A

1 Why does Caliban dislike Miranda? Give a quote from Act I, Scene 2 to support your answer.
2 What did Caliban say his dreams were about in Act III, Scene 2?

B

1 How do you think Caliban felt when Miranda called his native language 'gabble' in Act I, Scene 2, line 6?
2 Explain the meaning of 'Know thine own meaning' in Act I, Scene 2, line 6.
3 Explain what you think 'sweet airs' are in Act III, Scene 2, line 4.

C

1 What can the reader infer about the master/slave relationship between Prospero and Caliban in Act I, Scene 2?
2 Compare the way Caliban speaks, including the tone and his language, between Act I, Scene 2 and Act III, Scene 2. Explain why you think there is such a difference.
3 In which scene does Caliban seem the most free? Explain your answer.

Reminders of slavery

The poet James Berry was born in Jamaica in 1924, where he spent his childhood before travelling to the United States and later the United Kingdom, where he lived until his death. For Berry, aspects of the landscape of Jamaica always reminded him of the hard work of previous generations of slave workers.

- Consider how poets play with themes and conventions in a range of poetic forms
- Examine how writers use language and grammatical features to create meaning

Old Slave Villages

The windmills are dead
Their tombs are empty towers

Where high estate walls are broken down
Wire fences control the boundaries

5 Thatched slave shacks are gone
In their place – zinc houses, gardens

The great houses, now derelict,
Turned to school grounds – or hotels

The vast fields of sugar cane
10 Are pastures, with cattle grazing

The tombs of landscape windmills
Are broken empty towers.

JAMES BERRY

Talk about ...

- How important are landscapes to describing human histories?
- In what ways can poetry be effective in conveying feeling and emotion as well as fact?

Comprehension

1 How does the language the poet uses help to create a vividly negative image in the reader's mind?
2 Find an example of the use of a break-away dash in a sentence and explain how these are used.

1 The poem 'Old Slave Villages' mourns the past. How does the poem contribute to the ongoing discussion of the issues around exploitation and slave labour? Explain your answers.

 Stretch zone

Think about what you know about the history of your own country. Are there particular sites and settings that recall histories of oppression and hardship? Think of an artefact or a building that represents this history and write your own short poem or description.

What is it like to be in hiding?

This extract from *Incidents in the Life of a Slave Girl* was written by Harriet Jacobs in 1861. A slave for the first 27 years of her life, Harriet was born in Edenton, North Carolina, USA, where she was raised by her freed grandmother. Harriet learned to read, write and sew under her first mistress, and had hoped to be freed by her, but when her mistress died, Harriet was given to Dr James Norcom, who is called Dr Flint in the narrative. Although Dr Flint eventually freed Harriet's children, he was not a good master to Harriet. Eventually Harriet ran away and hid herself in the crawl space at her grandmother's house. From there, she waited for an opportunity to escape to the northern states of America, where slavery had been abolished.

- Examine closely how texts mirror the time and place in which they are written
- Look at a variety of texts and evaluate how writers develop ideas and themes in their writing

The loophole of retreat

A small shed had been added to my grandmother's house years ago. Some boards were laid across the joists at the top, and between these boards and the roof was a very small garret, never occupied by anything but rats and mice. It was a pent roof,
5   covered with nothing but shingles, according to the southern custom for such buildings. The garret was only nine feet long and seven wide. The highest part was three feet high, and sloped down abruptly to the loose board floor. There was no admission for either light or air. My uncle Phillip, who was a carpenter,
10 had very skilfully made a concealed trap-door, which communicated with a storeroom. [...]

To this hole I was conveyed as soon as I entered the house. The air was stifling; the darkness total. A bed had been spread on the floor. I could sleep quite comfortably on one side; but the
15 slope was so sudden that I could not turn on the other without hitting the roof. The rats and mice ran over my bed; but I was weary, and I slept such sleep as the wretched may. Morning came. I knew it only by the noises I heard; for in my small den day and night were all the same. I suffered for air even more
20 than light. But I was not comfortless. I heard the voices of my children. There was joy and there was sadness in the sound. It made my tears flow. How I longed to speak to them! I was eager to look on their faces; but there was no hole, no crack, through which I could peep.

Glossary

joist beam supporting a floor or ceiling
pent roof old term for a sloping roof
shingles wooden tiles used on walls and roofs

- Examine closely how texts mirror the time and place in which they are written
- Look at a variety of texts and evaluate how writers develop ideas and themes in their writing

25 This continued darkness was oppressive. It seemed horrible to sit or lie in a cramped position day after day, without one gleam of light. Yet I would have chosen this, rather than my lot as a slave, though white people considered it an easy one; and it was so compared with the fate of others. I was never cruelly

30 overworked; I was never lacerated with the whip from head to foot; I was never so beaten and bruised that I could not turn from one side to the other; I never had my heel-strings cut to prevent my running away; I was never chained to a log and forced to drag it about, while I toiled in the fields from morning

35 till night; I was never branded with hot iron, or torn by blood-hounds. On the contrary, I had always been kindly treated, and tenderly cared for, until I came into the hands of Dr Flint. I had never wished for freedom till then. [...]

My food was passed up to me through the trap-door my uncle

40 had contrived; and my grandmother, my uncle Phillip, and aunt Nancy would seize such opportunities as they could, to mount up there and chat with me at the opening. But of course this was not safe in the daytime. It must all be done in darkness. It was impossible for me to move in an erect position, but I

45 crawled about my den for exercise. One day I hit my head against something, and found it was a gimlet. My uncle had left it sticking there when he made the trap-door. I was as rejoiced as Robinson Crusoe could have been at finding such a treasure. It put a lucky thought into my head. I said to myself,

50 "Now I will have some light. Now I will see my children."

I did not dare to begin my work during the daytime, for fear of attracting attention. But I groped round; and having found the side next the street, where I could frequently see my children, I stuck the gimlet in and waited for evening. I bored three rows

55 of holes, one above another; then I bored out the interstices between. I thus succeeded in making one hole about an inch long and an inch broad. I sat by it till late into the night, to enjoy the little whiff of air that floated in. In the morning I watched for my children. The first person I saw in the street

60 was Dr Flint. I had a shuddering, superstitious feeling that it was a bad omen. Several familiar faces passed by. At last I heard the merry laugh of children, and presently two sweet little faces were looking up at me, as though they knew I was

Glossary

lacerate injure flesh by cutting or tearing it
toil hard, unpleasant work that makes you very tired
contrive find a clever way to do or make something
gimlet T-shaped tool with a screw tip for making holes
interstices spaces in between something

Language tip
An **abstract noun** describes an idea, quality or state rather than a physical object. They often end in one of the following common suffixes:

-ment, -ion, -ness, -ity, -ship, -dom

For example: 'freedom', 'oppression', 'conviction'.

- Examine closely how texts mirror the time and place in which they are written
- Look at a variety of texts and evaluate how writers develop ideas and themes in their writing

65 there, and were conscious of the joy they imparted. How I longed to *tell* them I was there!

The heat of my den was intense, for nothing but thin shingles protected me from the scorching summer's sun. But I had my consolations. Through my peeping-hole I could watch the children and when they were near enough, I could hear their
70 talk. Aunt Nancy brought me all the news she could hear at Dr Flint's. From her I learned that the doctor had written to New York to a colored woman who had been born and raised in our neighborhood. He offered her a reward if she could find out any thing about me. [...]

75 Autumn came, with a pleasant abatement of heat. My eyes had become accustomed to the dim light, and by holding my book or work in a certain position near the aperture I contrived to read and sew. That was a great relief to the tedious monotony of my life. But when winter came, the cold penetrated through
80 the thin shingle roof, and I was dreadfully chilled. The winters there are not so long, or so severe, as in northern latitudes; but the houses are not built to shelter from cold, and my little den was peculiarly comfortless. The kind grandmother brought me bed-clothes and warm drinks. Often I was obliged to lie in bed
85 all day to keep comfortable; but with all my precautions, my shoulders and feet were frostbitten. Oh, those long, gloomy days, with no object for my eye to rest upon, and no thoughts to occupy my mind, except the dreary past and the uncertain future! I was thankful when there came a day sufficiently mild
90 for me to wrap myself up and sit at the loophole to watch the passers by. Southerners have the habit of stopping and talking in the streets, and I heard many conversations not intended to meet my ears. I heard slave-hunters planning how to catch some poor fugitive. Several times I heard allusions to Dr Flint,
95 myself, and the history of my children. [...] Very rarely did any one suggest that I might be in the vicinity. Had the least suspicion rested on my grandmother's house, it would have been burned to the ground. But it was the last place they thought of. Yet there was no place, where slavery existed, that could have
100 afforded me so good a place of concealment.

From *Incidents in the Life of a Slave Girl* by HARRIET JACOBS

Glossary

abatement when something strong or harmful becomes less or dies down
aperture opening, hole or gap
vicinity area near or around a place

- Write using a variety of structures for different purposes
- Adapt writing style and register for intended audience and purpose
- Carry out comprehensive research on a range of topics

Comprehension

A 🧍

1 Describe the crawl space and its limitations in a few sentences.
2 Why doesn't Harriet let her children know that she is concealed in the roof?
3 What tortures does the writer describe that could happen to a slave?

B 🧍

1 Replace the following simple verbs in brackets with alternatives from the text.
   a He _____ (hid) himself behind the tree.
   b Her message was _____ (mimed) by gesture.
   c There was nothing _____ (made-up) about it.
   d The cat's leg was _____ (cut) by the wire.
   e He _____ (felt) around in the dark for the torch.
   f She felt _____ (it was her duty) to help them out.
2 Find five abstract nouns from the text and use them to write five sentences of your own.
3 Reread paragraph 2. How does the writer use a variety of sentence structures for different effects?

C 👀

1 Why do you think freedom is so important to Harriet, even though she is not as severely mistreated as other slaves?

Living without freedom

Write your own account of a day in the life of someone who is not at liberty to enjoy the freedoms most people take for granted. If you need inspiration for characters and settings for your account, you could research the work and projects of organizations like Amnesty International.

- Describe the situation. Make it realistic. Make detailed notes of the time and place, and the circumstances of your character's confinement or constraint.

- How would he or she feel? What would help a person get through such an ordeal? What sort of survival strategies would you or your character employ?

?

What would it be like to be in hiding, and in fear of your life if you were discovered? What would you do to protect yourself?

- Understand different points of view in a text
- Explain how an author develops character, setting and plot

An animal's perspective on freedom

The following extract is taken from *Watership Down* by Richard Adams. Watership Down is a hill in the north of Hampshire, England, near the area where the author grew up. It inspired Adams to write a story about a group of rabbits who set up a new settlement there after their original warren is destroyed by land developers.

Hazel, the chief rabbit, learns of a hutch of domestic rabbits at Nuthanger Farm. He and another young rabbit, Pipkin, make a visit to the farm to invite the rabbits there to join them. Hazel is not sure what he can expect of rabbits who have never experienced life in the wild, and who don't know how to cope with predators (*elil* in the rabbit language *Lapine*). But their most immediate problem is how to negotiate the farmyard cats.

Nuthanger Farm

The two rabbits began to wander among the outbuildings. At first they took care to remain under cover and were continually on the watch for cats. But they saw none and soon grew bolder, crossing open spaces and even stopping to nibble at dandelions
5   in the patches of weeds and rough grass.

Guided by scent, Hazel made his way to a low-roofed shed. The door was half open and he went through it with scarcely a pause at the brick threshold. Immediately opposite the door, on a broad wooden shelf – a kind of platform – stood a wire-
10   fronted hutch. Through the mesh he could see a brown bowl, some greenstuff and the ears of two or three rabbits. As he stared, one of the rabbits came close to the wire, looked out and saw him.

Beside the platform, on the near side, was an up-ended bale of
15   straw. Hazel jumped lightly on it and from there to the thick planks, which were old and soft-surfaced, dusty and covered with chaff. Then he turned back to Pipkin, waiting just inside the door.

"Pipkin," he said, "there's only one way out of this place. You'll
20   have to keep watching for cats or we may be trapped. Stay at the door and if you see a cat outside, tell me at once."

"Right, Hazel-rah," said Pipkin. "It's all clear at the moment."

- Understand different points of view in a text
- Explain how an author develops character, setting and plot

Hazel went to the side of the hutch. The wired front projected over the edge of the shelf so that he could neither reach it nor look in, but there was a knot-hole in one of the boards facing him and on the far side he could see a twitching nose.

"I am Hazel-rah," he said. "I have come to talk to you. Can you understand me?"

The answer was in strange but perfectly intelligible Lapine.

"Yes, we understand you. My name is Boxwood. Where do you come from?"

"From the hills. My friend and I live as we please, without men. We eat the grass, lie in the sun and sleep underground. How many are you?"

"Four. Bucks and does."

"Do you ever come out?"

"Yes, sometimes. A child takes us out and puts us in a pen on the grass."

"I have come to tell you about my warren. We need more rabbits. We want you to run away and join us."

"There's a wire door at the back of this hutch," said Boxwood. "Come down there: we can talk more easily."

The door was made of wire netting on a wooden frame, with two leather hinges to the uprights and a hasp and staple fastened with a twist of wire. Four rabbits were crowded against the wire, pressing their noses through the mesh. Two – Laurel and Clover – were short-haired black Angoras. The others, Boxwood and his doe Haystack, were black and white Himalayans.

Hazel began to speak about the life of the downs and the excitement and freedom enjoyed by wild rabbits. He spoke about the predicament of his warren in having no does and how he had come to look for some. "But," he said, "we don't want to steal your does. All four of you are welcome to join us, bucks and does alike. There's plenty for everyone on the hills." He went on to talk of the evening feed in the sunset and of early morning in the long grass.

Word origins

Lapine (n), fictional language that the rabbits speak in the novel. The word comes from the French word for rabbit, *le lapin*. Examples of some Lapine words in the extract:

- **elil** natural predators of rabbits: fox, stoat, weasel, cat, owl, human, etc.
- The suffix *-rah* means prince, lord or chief. ('Hazel-rah' is Hazel's title as chief rabbit.)

The hutch rabbits seemed at once bewildered and fascinated. Clover, the Angora doe, was clearly excited by Hazel's description and asked questions about the warren and the downs. It was

60 plain that they thought of their life in the hutch as dull but safe. They had heard about *elil* from some source or other and seemed sure that few wild rabbits survived for long. Hazel realized that although they were glad to talk and welcomed his visit because it brought a little excitement and change into their monotonous

65 life, it was not within their capacity to take a decision and act on it. They did not know how to make up their minds. To him and his companions, sensing and acting were second nature; but these rabbits had never had to act to save their lives or even to find a meal. If he was going to get any of them as far as the down

70 they would have to be urged. He sat quiet for a little, nibbling a patch of bran spilt on boards outside the hutch.

Then he said, "I must go back now to my friends in the hills; but we shall return. We shall come one night and when we do, any of you who wish will be free to come with us."

75 Boxwood was about to reply when suddenly Pipkin spoke from the floor. "Hazel, there's a cat in the yard outside!"

From *Watership Down* by RICHARD ADAMS

Glossary

buck male deer, rabbit or hare
doe female deer, rabbit or hare

The view from Watership Down, Hampshire

Comprehension

1 How does Hazel find the location of the hutch rabbits?

2 What role does Pipkin play in the visit to the farm?

3 What is Hazel's impression of the hutch rabbits?

4 What is the response of the hutch rabbits to the opportunity to join the group on Watership Down?

5 Explain Hazel's realization of the difference between his 'natural' life and those of the rabbits in captivity.

1 Hazel wants the rabbits at Nuthanger Farm to join his community of wild rabbits. Do you think these domesticated rabbits will be happier in the wild?

2 What might the price of freedom be for the rabbits?

3 Can it sometimes be better for animals to be kept in captivity?

- Carry out comprehensive research on a range of topics
- Make writing suitable for purpose and audience
- Understand different points of view in a text

Stretch zone

Find other fiction and non-fiction examples of writing that discuss the unique perspectives of species other than our own.

Why do you think it is important to consider the lives and perspectives of other species?

Writing from an animal's point of view

In his novel *Watership Down*, Richard Adams combined research, observation and creative invention to give as real an account as possible of what it might be like to be a rabbit in the wild.

Choose an animal that you are interested in. Write a short narrative about the world from your chosen animal's perspective.

- Create a sense of what your animal's life is like. Do they rule other animals, do they live in fear, and how do they co-operate together?
- Think of an exciting event or encounter to focus on.

7 The future

How do we see the future?

> All you who are dreamers too,
> Help me make
> Our world anew
> I reach out my hands to you
>
> From 'To You' by LANGSTON HUGHES

Talk about ...

- What are your dreams and visions for the future?
- Do you have any dreams for the future of the world?
- Is 'seeing the future' the same as planning for it and possibly contributing to a better outcome?

What do you think of when you think of the future? Across the world and over the centuries, people have had many different ideas and visions of the future, often inspired by hopes or dreams to create a better future for themselves and others.

In 1516, Thomas More wrote *Utopia*, which is about an island state in the future where people live communally in peace. Such idealistic visions of the future are called 'utopian'. The opposite of a utopia is a dystopia.

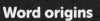

Word origins

utopia (n), comes from the ancient Greek prefix *ou-* for 'not' and the word *topos* for 'place'. Thomas More created this word as a pun, since the virtually identical prefix *eu-* means 'good'. More asks if such a 'good' place can ever really exist, or if it is a 'not-place'.

Its opposite, the word **dystopia** (n), is formed from the Greek prefix *dys-*, which means something bad, abnormal or difficult.

A powerful speech

This extract comes from the famous 'I Have a Dream' speech made by the American Civil Rights leader Martin Luther King, Jr. in Washington DC, USA, in 1963. It is one of the most passionate and powerful speeches of the twentieth century. Tragically, King was assassinated five years later in 1968.

King was a great speaker. Pay attention to his use of persuasive language and rhetorical devices, such as repetition, alliteration and metaphor.

- Distinguish between statements of fact and of opinion in texts to identify the viewpoint of the writer
- Identify evidence in a text about the environment, culture and social situation

I Have a Dream

I have a dream that one day this nation will rise up and live out the true meaning of its creed: 'We hold these truths to be self-evident, that all men are created equal.'

5 I have a dream that one day on the red hills of Georgia, the sons of former slaves and sons of former slave owners will be able to sit down together at the table of brotherhood.

I have a dream that one day even the state of
10 Mississippi, a state sweltering with the heat of injustice, sweltering with the heat of oppression, will be transformed into an oasis of freedom and justice.

I have a dream that my four little children
15 will one day live in a nation where they will not be judged by the color of their skin but by the content of their character. [...]

This is our hope, and this is the faith that I go back to the South with.

20 With this faith, we will be able to hew out of the mountain of despair a stone of hope. With this faith, we will be able to transform the jangling discords of our nation into a beautiful symphony of brotherhood. With this faith,
25 we will be able to work together, to pray together, to struggle together, to go to jail together, to stand up for freedom together, knowing that we will be free one day.

Martin Luther King, Jr., 28 August 1963

Comprehension

 A

1 What are the four points in Martin Luther King, Jr.'s dream?

2 In your own words, describe and explain the 'hope' and 'faith' which King wants to return home with.

 B

1 Which words are repeated the most in King's speech?

2 What is the effect of this repetition?

3 List the other rhetorical and poetic devices that King uses in his speech. Find examples of the devices used in the text and explain their effects.

 C

1 How do you think King wanted his audience to feel when he made the speech?

2 How does the 'I Have a Dream' speech make you feel? Discuss your answers with a partner.

3 What problems do you think King would want to solve if he made his speech today?

MARTIN LUTHER KING, JR.

- Understand how a point of view is conveyed in a text
- Explain how choosing certain language can enhance impact of writing

A poem about racial equality

The following poem was written in 1944 by the author of the opening quotation, the African-American poet Langston Hughes. He dreamed of a time when racial equality would exist in America, but he died before he saw his dream fulfilled.

I, too, sing America

I, too, sing America.

I am the darker brother.
They send me to eat in the kitchen
When company comes,
5   But I laugh,
And eat well,
And grow strong.

Tomorrow,
I'll be at the table
10 When company comes.
Nobody'll dare
Say to me,
'Eat in the kitchen',
Then.

15 Besides,
They'll see how beautiful I am
And be ashamed –

I, too, am America.

LANGSTON HUGHES

Langston Hughes, around 1928

Comprehension

 A

1 The phrase 'I, too' means 'I, as well as …' Who else is the poet thinking of?
2 Where is the poet sent to eat?
3 What is his response to this treatment?

 B

1 Find examples of repetition used in the poem. What effect does this have?
2 How does the use of free verse help to emphasize the poem's message?
3 What does the poet mean by 'I'll be at the table'?
4 Find examples of enjambment and comment on its role in the poem.

 C

1 How is the poem optimistic about the future?
2 Do you think we have reached 'Tomorrow' yet? What things still need to change?

Language tip

Free verse is poetry that doesn't have a particular rhyme scheme or structure like other poems. It follows the natural rhythms of speech.

Enjambment means the continuation of a sentence from one line of poetry to the next. It allows a thought or phrase to be unrestricted by the end of the poem's line.

A promise to protect the planet

The following extract is from a poem by spoken word artist Kathy Jetñil-Kijiner, who comes from the Marshall Islands. The poem is addressed to the poet's baby daughter. It was performed at the opening ceremony of the 2014 United Nations Climate Summit to encourage all those attending to work towards protecting her daughter's future.

Like other island states, the Marshall Islands are vulnerable to rising sea levels and extreme weather events caused by rising global temperatures.

- Consider how poets play with themes and conventions in a range of poetic forms
- Examine closely how texts mirror the time and place in which they are written

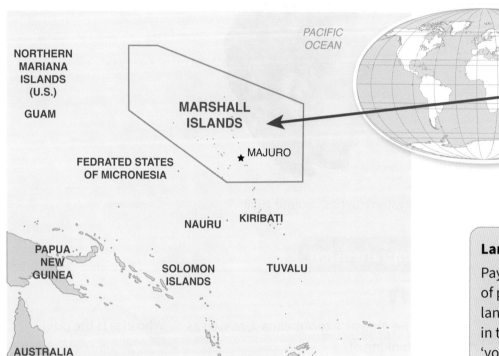

Language tip

Pay attention to the use of pronouns that make language more inclusive, as in the examples 'we will' or 'you'll see'.

Talk about ...

- Who are the most influential climate activists where you live?
- What (if any) effects of climate change are evident in your country or region?
- Can you think of any other works of poetry that express concerns about climate change?

Kathy Jetñil-Kijiner and her family at the opening ceremony of the UN Climate Summit in New York in September 2014

- Consider how poets play with themes and conventions in a range of poetic forms
- Examine closely how texts mirror the time and place in which they are written

from **Dear Matafele Peinam**

i take this moment
to apologize to you
we are drawing the line here

5 because baby we are going to fight
your mommy daddy
bubu jimma your country and president too
we will all fight

and even though there are those
hidden behind platinum titles
10 who like to pretend
that we don't exist
that the marshall islands
tuvalu
kiribati
15 maldives
and typhoon haiyan in the philippines
and floods of pakistan, algeria, colombia
and all the hurricanes, earthquakes, and
tidalwaves
20 didn't exist

still
there are those
who see us

hands reaching out
25 fists raising up
banners unfurling
megaphones booming
and we are
canoes blocking coal ships
30 we are
the radiance of solar villages
we are

the rich clean soil of the farmer's past
we are
35 petitions blooming from teenage fingertips
we are
families biking, recycling, reusing
engineers dreaming, designing, building
artists painting, dancing, writing
40 and we are spreading the word

and there are thousands out on the street
marching with signs
hand in hand
chanting for change NOW

45 and they're marching for you, baby
they're marching for us

because we deserve to do more than just
survive
we deserve
50 to thrive

dear matafele peinam,

you are eyes heavy
with drowsy weight
so just close those eyes, baby
55 and sleep in peace

because we won't let you down
you'll see

KATHY JETÑIL-KIJINER

Comprehension

1 Who is the poem directly addressed to, and who is it indirectly addressed to?

2 What is the poet apologizing for?

3 What is the promise the poem concludes on?

1 **a** Find two verb phrases in the poem that use personal pronouns to introduce inclusive actions.

   b Now write two sentences of your own using the same two verb phrases.

2 Explain the meaning (literal and extended/metaphorical) of the following phrases in this poem:

   a 'drawing the line'

   b 'platinum titles'

   c 'radiance of solar villages'

   d 'petitions blooming from teenager fingertips'

3 Find verbs from the text to replace the alternatives in brackets:

   a megaphones (that are loud)

   b hands (extending) out

   c (repeating) the word

   d (shouting) for change NOW

   Now write sentences using these verb phrases from the poem.

1 Do you think this poem would have had more effect on the audience at the UN Climate Summit than a speech on the same topic? Why?

- Evaluate and compare a range of texts by re-reading and watching recorded or live versions
- Examine how a writer's use of language and grammatical features creates effects and meaning

 Stretch zone

Look online for the video presentation at the UN Climate Summit and watch the full performance. Compose a response to Kathy Jetñil-Kijiner and her delegation from the Marshall Islands.

Aerial view of the Marshall Islands

A story about time travel

The following extract is from *The Time Machine* written by the British novelist H.G. Wells in 1895. The account is from the final part of the novel in which the narrator describes a desolate and chilling landscape inhabited by terrifying creatures that he encounters at different times far into the future.

The narrator is the inventor who is addressing his colleagues on his return.

> - Examine and discuss a wide range of texts
> - Examine closely how texts mirror the time and place in which they are written

My return

I stopped and sat upon the Time Machine, looking around. The sky was no longer blue. Ahead, it was inky dark, and out of the blackness shone brightly and steadily the white stars. Overhead it was starless and a deep red and behind it
5 was glowing scarlet where lay the huge sun, red and motionless. The rocks about me were of a harsh reddish colour, and all the trace of life that I could see at first was the intensely green vegetation that covered every projecting point. It was the same rich green that one sees on plants which grow in a
10 perpetual twilight.

The Time Machine was standing on a sloping beach. The sea stretched to a sharp bright horizon against the pale sky. There were no waves, for not a breath of wind was stirring. Only a slow swell, which rose and fell like a gentle breathing, showed
15 that the sea was still living. Where the water sometimes broke was a thick incrustation of salt, which appeared pink under the lurid sky. The air forced me to breathe very fast which reminded me of my only experience of mountaineering.

Looking round me again, I saw that what I had taken to be a
20 reddish mass of rock was moving slowly towards me. It was a monstrous crab-like creature. Can you imagine a crab as large as that table, with its many legs moving slowly, its big claws swaying, its long antennae waving and feeling, and its eyes on stalks gleaming at you? Its back was covered with ugly
25 lumps and a greenish incrustation. I could see its complicated mouth flickering as it moved.

Cover from a 1960s comic of *The Time Machine*

- Examine and discuss a wide range of texts
- Examine closely how texts mirror the time and place in which they are written

As I stared at this sinister creature crawling towards me, I felt a tickling on my cheek as though a fly had lighted there. I tried to brush it away with my hand, but in a moment it had
30 returned, and almost immediately came another by my ear. As I tried again to brush it away, I caught something threadlike which was drawn swiftly out of my hand. In fright, I turned and saw that I had grasped the antenna of another monster crab that stood just behind me. Its evil eyes were wriggling on
35 their stalks, its mouth was all alive with appetite, and its vast claws, smeared with an algal slime, were descending upon me.

In a moment my hand was on the lever of my Time Machine, and I had placed a month between myself and these monsters. But I was still on the same beach, and I saw them distinctly;
40 dozens of them were crawling in the sombre light. I cannot convey the sense of abominable desolation that hung over the world. The red eastern sky, the blackness northward, the dead sea, the stony beach crawling with these slow-stirring monsters, the poisonous-looking green of the plants, the thin air that
45 hurt my lungs: all contributed to an appalling effect. I moved on a hundred years, and all was still the same.

I then travelled on a thousand years or more, drawn on by the mystery of the earth's fate, watching with a strange fascination the sun grow larger and duller in the westward sky, and the
50 life of the old earth ebb away. At last, more than thirty million years hence, the huge red-hot dome of the sun had come to obscure nearly a tenth part of the dark sky. Then I stopped once more, for the crawling multitude of crabs had disappeared, and the red beach seemed lifeless. Now it was flecked with
55 white and a bitter cold assailed me as white flakes came eddying down. There were fringes of ice along the sea margin, but the main expanse of that salt ocean, all bloody under the eternal sunset, was still unfrozen.

I looked about me to see if any traces of animal life remained
60 but I saw nothing moving, in earth or sky or sea. The green slime on the rocks alone testified that life was not extinct. Suddenly I noticed that the circular outline of the sun had changed. For a minute perhaps I stared aghast at the blackness that was creeping over the day, and then I realized that an eclipse was beginning.
65 Either the moon or the planet Mercury was passing across the

Glossary

antennae thin, whiskery feelers, or sensory receptors, on either side of the heads of crustaceans, insects and butterflies

algal adjective form of algae (plants that grow in water)

aghast shocked and horrified at something terrible or unpleasant

eclipse blocking of the sun's or moon's light when the Moon or Earth is in the way

- Understand the meaning and effect of new and unfamiliar words

sun's disk. The darkness grew; a cold wind began to blow in gusts, and the white flakes in the air increased in number.

From the edge of the sea came a ripple and whisper. Beyond these lifeless sounds the world was silent. Utterly silent. All the
70 sounds of man – the bleating of sheep, the cries of birds, the hum of insects, the stir that makes the background of our lives – all that was over. As the darkness thickened, the snow flakes grew more abundant and the cold of the air more intense. At last, one by one, swiftly, one after the other, the white peaks
75 of the distant hills vanished into blackness. The breeze rose to a moaning wind. I saw the black central shadow of the eclipse sweeping towards me. In another moment all was rayless obscurity. The sky was absolutely black.

A horror of this great darkness came on me. I was cold to my
80 marrow, and the pain I felt in breathing overcame me. Then in the sky appeared the edge of the sun again as a red-hot arc. I got off my Time Machine to recover myself. As I stood sick and confused, I saw again a thing moving towards the shore. It was a round thing, the size of a football perhaps, and tentacles trailed
85 down from it. It seemed black against the blood-red water and it was hopping fitfully about. I felt I was fainting. A terrible dread of lying helpless in that remote and awful twilight sustained me while I clambered upon the saddle of my Time Machine.

Then, gentlemen, I returned.

From *The Time Machine* by H.G. WELLS

Glossary

marrow soft substance inside bones

arc curve; part of the circumference of a circle

tentacle long, flexible part of the body of an octopus used for feeling, grasping things or moving

113

- Write a range of different fiction genres and poetry
- Use increasingly complex texts as a model for own writing, responding to new genres

Comprehension

1 What are the dominant colours used to describe the landscape?
2 Why was the inventor reminded of his mountaineering experience?
3 What was the thread-like thing that the inventor caught in his hand?
4 How far into the future does the inventor travel each time?
5 Explain why the inventor felt such 'horror' in the final paragraph.

1 Choose three descriptive passages that focus on the details of the physical geography, solar system and natural life (hard sci-fi).
2 List the descriptive words that communicate an emotional response (soft sci-fi).
3 How important is it to the impact of the story that we experience both types of sci-fi?

1 What do you think about the concept of a time machine as a form of transport?
2 Are there other ways of imagining the changes that might happen (or have happened) over time in a particular landscape?

Writing science fiction

Now it's your turn to create a work of science fiction. Use your imagination to create a version of the future through an imagined scene or encounter that makes use of some of the conventions of the science fiction genre that you are now familiar with.

- Think of a frightening and chilling scenario, or a utopian vision. Your vision of the future could be a short story or the introductory chapter to a novel if you prefer.
- Concentrate on your use of descriptive vocabulary, so that the reader can imagine what it would be like to be there.

Learning tip

Science fiction (sci-fi for short) can be divided into two broad categories:
- **hard sci-fi** is inspired by technical or scientific fact
- **soft sci-fi** is inspired by the social sciences and arts.

Most effective science or speculative fiction is a mixture of both.

Climate fiction (or cli-fi for short) is a form of science fiction that features a changed or changing climate as a major plot device.

Have people's perceptions or predictions about the future changed over the last century?

A story about a robot

Russian-born American writer Isaac Asimov's stories highlight the possible, if unexpected, results of humanity's technological advances. This extract is from a short story written in 1941 that was published in a collection of stories called *I, Robot*.

In the story, Cutie the robot becomes convinced that he is superior to humans. He must take control of the ship for he knows only he can save it. Without the crew being aware of it, Cutie is following the first law of robotics which is embedded in his programming: a robot must not harm or allow a human to be harmed. In the extract below, Cutie uses reason to convince himself that his action of taking over the ship is justified.

- Compare a wide range of texts on the same theme
- Understand the meaning and effect of new and unfamiliar words

A superior robot

Powell stood up and seated himself at the table's edge next to the robot. He felt a sudden strong sympathy for this strange machine. It was not at all like the ordinary robot, attending to his specialized task at the station with the intensity of a
5 deeply engraved positronic path.

He placed a hand upon Cutie's steel shoulder and the metal was cold and hard to the touch.

"Cutie," he said, "I'm going to try to explain something to you. You're the first robot who's ever exhibited curiosity as to
10 his own existence – and I think the first that's really intelligent enough to understand the world outside. Here, come with me."

The robot rose up smoothly and his thickly sponge-rubber-soled feet made no noise as he followed Powell. The Earthman touched a button and a square section of the wall flickered
15 aside. The thick, clear glass revealed space – star-speckled.

"I've seen that in the observation ports in the engine room," said Cutie.

"I know," said Powell.
20 "What do you think it is?"

"Exactly what it seems – a black material just beyond this glass that is spotted with little gleaming dots. I know that our director
25 sends out beams to some of these

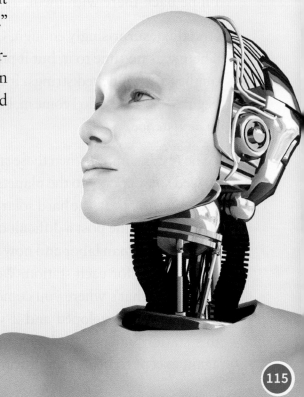

dots, always to the same ones – and also that these dots shift and that the beams shift with them. That is all."

"Good! Now I want you to listen carefully. The blackness
30 is emptiness – vast emptiness stretching out infinitely. The little, gleaming dots are huge masses of energy-filled matter. They are globes, some of them millions of miles in diameter – and for comparison, this station is only one mile across. They seem so tiny because they are incredibly far off."

"The dots to which our energy beams are directed are nearer
35 and much smaller. They are cold and hard, and human beings like myself live upon their surface – many billions of them. It is from one of these worlds that Donovan and I come. Our beams feed these worlds energy drawn from one of those huge incandescent globes that happens to be near us.
40 We call that globe the Sun and it is on the other side of the station where you can't see it."

Cutie remained motionless before the port, like a steel statue. His head did not turn as he spoke, "Which particular dot of light do you claim to come from?"

45 Powell searched, "There it is. The very bright one in the corner. We call it Earth." He grinned, "Good old Earth. There are three billions of us there, Cutie – and in about two weeks I'll be back there with them."

And then, surprisingly enough, Cutie hummed abstractedly.
50 There was no tune to it, but it possessed a curious twanging quality as of plucked strings. It ceased as suddenly as it had begun, "But where do I come in, Powell? You haven't explained *my* existence."

"The rest is simple. When these stations were first established
55 to feed solar energy to the planets, they were run by humans. However, the heat, the hard solar radiations, and the electron storms made the post a difficult one. Robots were developed to replace human labor and now only two human executives are required for each station. We are trying to replace even
60 those, and that's where you come in. You're the highest type of robot ever developed and if you show the ability to run this station independently, no human need ever come here again except to bring parts for repairs."

Glossary

incandescent giving out light when heated; shining
executives senior people in authority

Learning tip

When you read a new extract for the first time, try to get into the habit of noting down anything you notice about language features, character, structure, and general ideas and themes. This will help you to gain an overall understanding of what is happening in the extract so you are fully prepared for the Comprehension questions.

- Compare a wide range of texts on the same theme

Powell returned to the table and polished an apple upon his
65 sleeve before biting into it.

The red glow of the robot's eyes held him. "Do you expect me,"
said Cutie slowly, "to believe any such complicated, implausible
hypothesis as you have just outlined? What do you take me for?"

Powell sputtered apple fragments onto the table and turned
70 red. "Why ... it wasn't a hypothesis. Those were facts."

Cutie sounded grim, "Globes of energy millions of miles across!
Worlds with three billion humans on them! Infinite emptiness!
Sorry, Powell, but I don't believe it. I'll puzzle this thing out
for myself. Good-bye."

75 He turned and stalked out of the room. He brushed past Michael
Donovan on the threshold with a grave nod and passed down
the corridor, oblivious to the astounded stare that followed him.

Mike Donovan rumpled his red hair and shot an annoyed
glance at Powell, "What was that walking junk yard talking
80 about? What doesn't he believe?"

Glossary

implausible not reasonable, plausible or convincing

The other dragged at his mustache bitterly. "He's a skeptic," was the bitter response. "He doesn't believe we made him or that Earth exists or space or stars."

"Sizzling Saturn, we've got a lunatic robot on our hands."

85 "He says he's going to figure it all out for himself."

"Well, now," said Donovan sweetly, "I do hope he'll condescend to explain it all to me after he's puzzled everything out." [...]

He seated himself with a jerk and drew a paper-backed mystery novel 90 out of his inner jacket pocket, "That robot gives me the willies anyway – too inquisitive!"

From *Reason* by Isaac Asimov

- Compare a wide range of texts on the same theme
- Examine how a writer's use of language and grammatical features creates effects and meaning

UK	USA
labour	labor
moustache	mustache
sceptic	skeptic

Glossary

skeptic (US) / sceptic (UK) someone who doubts things that others believe

the willies strong feeling of nervous discomfort

Stretch zone

Imagine what might happen in the story after the end of the extract. Write two or three paragraphs and try to include some of the literary devices focused on in this section.

Comprehension

1 Why does Powell have sympathy for Cutie?

2 Why does Powell describe Cutie as a 'skeptic'?

3 In lines 49–52, the writer describes Cutie's humming. What effect does his description of the robot performing such a 'human' action create?

4 Why is Donovan alarmed by Cutie's level of enquiry and 'inquisitiveness'?

1 Find some examples in the text of alliteration, assonance and consonance.

2 Now write two examples of your own of each of these literary devices. Use the examples from the text to help you.

1 What do you think is the difference between how a human can think and the way that a robot thinks?

2 Work with a partner to make a list of how artificial intelligence can help you in your everyday life.

3 How would you like artifical intelligence to help you in the future?

Language tip

Alliteration, **assonance** and **consonance** help to emphasize concepts and make passages of text more memorable:

- **alliteration** is when two or more words begin with the same consonant sound, for example, 'Sizzling Saturn'
- **assonance** is the repetition of vowel sounds in a sentence, for example, 'The early bird catches the worm'
- **consonance** is a repeated consonant sound at the end or in the middle of words, for example, 'All's well that ends well'.

Researching artificial intelligence

Do your own research into some form of artificial intelligence (AI for short).

You are going to give a brief presentation on your chosen form of AI at a youth summit focusing on how the world will change over the next 50 years. Some people attending the summit will be there in person, and some will be attending online.

You might choose to research facial recognition for security, autocorrect to help you with spelling and grammar, self-driving cars, robopets, or something entirely different!

- Begin your presentation by establishing a clear definition of artificial intelligence.
- What advantages could the form of AI you have researched bring to human society? Could there be any disadvantages?
- What do you think are the limits of AI and its application to our future human society?
- Consider how you will present your findings at the summit. Will you need to create slides? What images will you use to make it visually engaging? How will you ensure that the attendees in person and online feel equally involved?
- Get into groups of three or four and give your presentations. Allow enough time to ask one another questions at the end.

Once you have all given your presentations, open up a discussion in your group about your own personal opinions of the future of AI. Is there a consensus, or do you all feel differently?

- Make sure text type, structure and style are suitable for the audience
- Carry out comprehensive research using a range of sources
- Use literary and rhetorical devices to enhance the impact of writing
- Use verbal and non-verbal techniques when presenting information to aid an audience's understanding
- Listen and respond politely to opposing views in discussions

Are robopets the future?

Write about your visions of the future

In this unit, you have read a range of different texts in many different styles and genres.

These include speeches and poetry that present people's hopes for the future in the face of significant challenges through:

- dreams of achieving racial equality in society (Martin Luther King, Jr. and Langston Hughes)
- a promise to fight for the future of the planet (Kathy Jetñil-Kijiner).

Science fiction is an exciting genre for both predicting and analyzing our fears and fascination for the future. Such stories are often based on the use of new technologies, such as:

- travelling through time to other civilizations, and seeing a desolate future world (H.G. Wells's *The Time Machine*)
- a futuristic robot who wants to take control (Isaac Asimov's *Reason*).

Now it's your turn to come up with a vision for the future. It could be 50 years from now, or 500 – it's up to you.

Plan your writing carefully. Refer to the extracts in this unit to inspire you and perhaps consider the following:

- What things have changed in this future society compared to today?
- What technological advances have there been?
- What is the state of the planet – are things better than today or worse?

Share your finished writing with a partner and comment on each other's writing. Give two things you like about it and one thing you think your partner could do to improve or extend their work.

- Compare and contrast a wide range of texts on the same theme
- Look at how texts are structured and presented in order to influence the reader's point of view
- Carry out comprehensive research using a range of sources
- Apply knowledge of vocabulary, grammar and structure to influence the reader's point of view

http://www.evlad.com

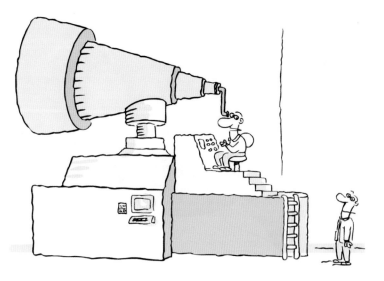

"No...I can not see the future..."

8 A dream of flying

Why do we dream of flying?

> 'Up, up and away in my beautiful, my beautiful balloon'
>
> From the song 'Up, Up and Away', written by JIMMY WEBB

Talk about ...

- Why do we dream of flying?
- Do humans envy birds because they can fly?
- What does it feel like to fly in a flying machine?
- Do you know any stories about flying?

From very early times, our ancestors must have watched birds and insects flying in the sky and dreamed of what it would be like to be able to fly. Perhaps they dreamed of having the wings of a bird, or saw flying as the ultimate dream of escape. The idea of human flight did not become a real possibility until the end of the nineteenth century, when the first 'flying machines' made their test flights. Even now, when passenger aircraft fly all over the world, people still want to fly like birds and practise sports like abseiling, hang gliding and bungee jumping.

- Find evidence in a text about the environment, culture and social situation
- Discuss new and unfamiliar words
- Read a variety of texts and evaluate how writers develop ideas and themes in their writing

The tragedy of Icarus

The myth of Daedalus who built wings for himself and his son Icarus is a great story of human inventiveness and failure. It was told, probably not for the first time, by the great Roman writer Ovid, who was born in 43 BCE. Since then, the story has been told and retold all over the world, and it continues to be an inspiration for writers and artists right up to the present day.

Talos's soul took the form of a partridge

Daedalus and Icarus

In Athens, and throughout ancient Greece, Daedalus was a renowned craftsman and inventor. He had taken on his nephew, Talos, as an apprentice, but by the age of twelve Talos had surpassed his master in skill. One
5   day Talos studied the spine of a fish, copied it in iron, and so invented the first saw. He also invented the potter's wheel and a compass for marking out circles. Instead of being delighted at his nephew's inventions, Daedalus became jealous.

His jealousy grew and festered inside him. At last, as Talos's
10 skills developed, Daedalus's jealousy became unbearable to him and he devised an evil plan. He invited Talos up to the roof of Athene's temple in the Acropolis to see the wonderful views from the top. Talos went happily with his uncle. Daedalus did indeed show him the impressive view, but as the boy gazed
15 entranced at the temples far below, Daedalus pushed him over the edge. Daedalus tried to bury his nephew's body secretly, but he was found out and banished. Talos was buried where he fell and his soul flew off in the form of a partridge.

Daedalus fled to Crete with his son, Icarus, where for a while
20 they lived in peace. One day, King Minos of Crete called Daedalus to him. He wanted him to build a labyrinth in the cellars of his grand palace. Only Daedalus was skilled enough to design a maze of tunnels which no one else could ever find the way out of. Daedalus did as the king asked. He laboured
25 for many months and the cruel tyrant King Minos was pleased with the result. The labyrinth was to be the prison of the Minotaur, an evil monster with the head of a bull and the body of a man. The Minotaur was fed with young men and women who were sent from Athens to supply its greedy appetite.

Glossary

renowned famous or celebrated

surpass do or be better than others

fester (of a negative feeling or problem) become worse or more intense

devise invent or plan something

entrance delight or enchant someone

perch rest or sit on the edge of something

- Find evidence in a text about the environment, culture and social situation
- Read a variety of texts and evaluate how writers develop ideas and themes in their writing

30 Daedalus now wanted to leave Crete, but King Minos would not let him leave.

"You made the labyrinth and are the only one who knows the way out. I cannot let you go," he said.

So once more, Daedalus had to flee his home. But it was not 35 easy to escape from Crete, because it was an island, and King Minos kept all his ships under military guard, offering a large reward to anyone who captured Daedalus or his son. Daedalus decided that the only escape was through the air: he and his son would fly to safety. He set to work to make two pairs of 40 wings from birds' feathers which he and Icarus collected each day. He painstakingly threaded them all together, and secured them with wax. After many weeks, the wings were ready. He tied the wings onto the shoulders and arms of 45 both himself and his son.

"My dear Icarus," he said, holding his shoulders and looking into his eyes. "You must obey this one rule. Do not soar too high, or the sun will melt the wax, and do 50 not swoop too low, or the sea will wet the feathers, and you will fall. Do you promise me?"

"I promise, Father," the excited boy replied.

Together they took off and, flapping their 55 giant feathered wings, they flew over Crete. Fishermen, shepherds and ploughmen gazed upwards at what they thought were angels flying in the sky. Icarus was enjoying himself greatly in the warm currents of air. Rejoicing 60 in the exhilarating sweep of his wings, he forgot his father's warning, and in a great rush of joy, he soared up towards the sun. As they left Crete behind, Daedalus turned to make sure Icarus was following him, but 65 his son had disappeared. He looked down to the sea below him and saw scattered feathers floating on the turquoise water.

The Minotaur, painted by George Frederic Watts in 1885

123

Daedalus circled around the spot where Icarus had fallen until his son's body rose to the surface. He carried his drowned boy to a nearby island, now called Icaria, where he buried him with many tears.

70

Perched on a tree as Daedalus wept was a partridge cooing triumphantly to itself.

- Find evidence in a text about the environment, culture and social situation
- Identify and evaluate how writers develop ideas and themes in their writing
- Participate fully in discussions
- Present personal opinions clearly and succinctly with confidence

Comprehension

A

1 What was so special and threatening about Talos?
2 What is a Minotaur, and why is it considered to be a monster?
3 Why was Daedalus so anxious to leave the island of Crete?
4 What were the risks associated with the attachment of the wings?

B

1 Which elements of the story are typical of the story structure of myths? Find examples in the story of:

   a applying oneself to a trade or task to do well
   b the setting of rules or conditions that must be obeyed
   c a tragic outcome when rules are not followed
   d symbolic human–animal shapeshifters

   Write an extended explanation of two key examples from the above to explain how the elements of a myth contribute to the tragic story of Daedalus and Icarus.

C

1 What does the metaphor of flying too close to the sun mean to you?

Learning tip
Mythological stories (**myths** for short) often communicate a moral or a message, like a warning not to take risks or do the wrong thing by your family and community.

These kinds of stories are usually tightly structured, with clearly defined characters, settings, plot lines and a central conflict that is followed by an outcome or resolution.

Write your own version of a popular myth

Choose a fable, myth or folk tale you know well and update the story by giving it a more contemporary feel.

- Describe the setting and the characters. You could use a photograph or a scene from a film as a model for your retelling of the story.
- How does the issue in the original story relate to the problems that people face today? You may need to change some of the details to make it relevant.
- Remember to keep some details from the original version to show the connection.

An artist's perspective on the story of Icarus

The painting below is called *Landscape with the Fall of Icarus*. It was painted in about 1555 by the Netherlandish artist Pieter Bruegel, known as Pieter Bruegel the Elder, who came from a famous family of artists. This scene would have looked like a painting of daily life to someone living in Flanders (modern-day Belgium) at the time.

Landscape with the Fall of Icarus, painted in about 1555 by Pieter Bruegel the Elder

- Find evidence in a text about the environment, culture and social situation
- Continue to improve accuracy of grammar, language and structure in writing
- Proofread and edit writing
- Use increasingly complex texts as a model for own writing
- Participate fully in discussions

Comprehension

1 Describe what is happening in the painting.
2 Who/what is in the foreground?
3 Where is Icarus, and how is this significant?
4 What is the reaction to this of the other people in the painting?

1 Why do you think artists decide to represent classical myths in their own time and society?
2 How could the moral of the story of Icarus be updated to a story set in today's world?

A poet's interpretation of the Icarus painting

The twentieth-century American poet William Carlos Williams wrote the following poem after seeing the painting *Landscape with the Fall of Icarus* that you have just been looking at.

- Consider how poets play with themes and conventions
- Know how punctuation can be used to convey meaning in creative texts
- Examine how a writer's use of language and grammatical features creates effect and meaning

Landscape with the Fall of Icarus

According to Brueghel
when Icarus fell it was spring

a farmer was ploughing
his field
5   the whole pageantry

of the year was
awake tingling
near

the edge of the sea
10   concerned
with itself

sweating in the sun
that melted
the wings' wax

15   unsignificantly
off the coast
there was

a splash quite unnoticed
this was
20   Icarus drowning.

WILLIAM CARLOS WILLIAMS

Comprehension

1 How does the title reflect the focus of the poem?

2 What is significant about the season of spring? Which words and phrases help to create this atmosphere?

1 a In what ways are 'unsignificantly' and 'unnoticed' key words in the poem?

  b The correct negative prefix for 'significantly' is *in-* not *un-*. Why do you think the poet chose to use *un-*?

2 Why do you think the writer chose to use enjambment in this poem?

1 Do you think it is strange that even in the twenty-first century we still like to tell stories based on ancient myths and legends? Discuss in reference to the story of Icarus, as well as other examples that you know of.

Language tip
There is no punctuation in the poem apart from the final full stop. The way the lines lead into one another without punctuation is an example of **enjambment**.

Who invented flight?

In past centuries, long before the invention of aeroplanes and flying machines, people experimented with designs and ideas which went way beyond building bird wings like Daedalus's.

The most famous of these designs are by the great Italian artist–scientist Leonardo da Vinci, who lived between 1452 and 1519. He studied the flight of birds and designed a range of devices, including a kind of helicopter, a parachute and a hang glider. More than four centuries after it was designed, Leonardo da Vinci's hang glider was constructed and flown.

French engineer Alexandre Goupil built Goupil's sesquiplane in 1883, and Jean-Marie Le Bris designed *L'Albatros artificiel* ('The Artificial Albatross') in 1856, a glider inspired by the shape of an albatross. There were many inventions and a number of them actually worked but weren't further developed.

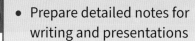

- Prepare detailed notes for writing and presentations
- Use verbal and non-verbal techniques when presenting information to aid understanding
- Select the most appropriate forms for media and multimedia elements in a presentation

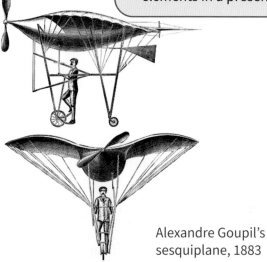

Alexandre Goupil's sesquiplane, 1883

L'Albatros artificiel, built by Le Bris in 1856

One of Leonardo da Vinci's flying machines

Present your favourite flying invention!

There are accounts of human flight going back thousands of years. But it wasn't until the twentieth century that real advances in flight machines were made.

- Prepare a presentation on your favourite early idea or invention of a flying machine. What inspired the inventor? Did it become the prototype for something that came later?
- Provide visual support in the form of diagrams and photos.
- Deliver your presentation to your group and ask for feedback.

A poem about birds

The following poem was written by the Romanian poet, Marin Sorescu, while Romania was under the repressive regime of dictator Nicolae Ceaușescu in the second half of the twentieth century. Sorescu's collection of poems called *Censored Poems* was not released for publication until after Ceaușescu's death.

- Identify the viewpoint of the writer, and how meaning can be conveyed
- Participate fully in discussions
- Present personal opinions clearly and succinctly with confidence
- Examine how a writer's use of language and grammatical features creates effect and meaning

Playing Icarus

I went begging to the birds
And each of them gave me
A feather.

5 A high one from the vulture,
A red one from the bird of paradise,
A green one from the humming-bird,
A talking one from the parrot,
A shy one from the ostrich –
Oh, what wings I've made for myself.
10

I've attached them to my soul
And I've started to fly.
High flight of the vulture,
Red flight of the bird of paradise,
15 Green flight of the humming-bird,
Talking flight of the parrot,
Shy flight of the ostrich –
Oh, how I've flown!

MARIN SORESCU

Comprehension

1 What is the meaning of the poem's title, 'Playing Icarus'?

2 What is the significance of being given one feather from each bird?

3 What kind of flying is the poet talking about?

1 How is repetition used to structure this poem?

1 How does the title of the collection of poems, and further information about the experiences of living under a repressive regime, affect how you interpret this poem?

A hummingbird

Language tip
Repetition is a simple but effective technique that can be used to create a sense of rhythm, deepen meaning, or add emphasis in a poem.

Stretch zone
Write your own short poem about a bird who gave the poet a feather.

A pilot's adventures

- Find evidence in a text about the environment, culture and social situation

Antoine de Saint-Exupéry worked for the French airmail service and later the French Air Force in the Second World War.

He used his own experience travelling in Europe, Africa and South America as the basis for his fictional writing. In these accounts, he describes the early days of aviation, when aeroplanes had an open cockpit and pilots were exposed to the elements, often flying solo over difficult and dangerous terrain. Before air travel was a common experience, few people had seen what the landscape looked like from the air – not even in films and photographs.

In the following short extracts from the novel *Southern Mail*, published in 1929, Jacques Bernis, the pilot in the story, starts out by describing his impression of the landscape below.

?

Have you ever flown in a plane? How did your experience compare to Antoine de Saint-Exupéry's account?

Antoine de Saint-Exupéry

Flying into Alicante

From up there the earth had looked bare and dead; but as the plane loses altitude, it robes itself in colours. The woods spread out their quilts, the hills and valleys rise and fall in waves, like someone breathing. A mountain over which he flies swells like
5 some recumbent giant's breast, almost grazing his wing-tip.

Now close, like a torrent under a bridge, the earth begins its mad acceleration. The ordered world becomes a landslide, as houses and villages are torn from the smooth horizon and swept away behind him. The landing strip of Alicante rises,
10 tilts, then steadies into place. The wheels graze and then grind into it as on a whet-stone.

As Bernis climbs out of the cockpit, his legs feel heavy. For a second he closes his eyes, his head still full of sky and the roar of his engine, his limbs still quivering from the vibrations of
15 his machine. Then, entering the office, he slowly sits down, pushes aside the ink well and several books, and pulls the flight plan for Plane 612 towards him.

Toulouse–Alicante: 5 hours, 15 minutes flying time.

Motor: nothing to report.

20 Plane: slight tilt to starboard.

He lays down the pen and thinks, "I'm tired," as the same vision hovers before his gaze. An amber light falling on a radiant landscape. Meadows and well-ploughed fields. A village off to the right, to the left a tiny flock of sheep, and covering them
25 all the blue vault of heaven. "A house," thinks Bernis. He remembers having felt, with a sudden certitude, that this countryside, this sky, this earth were all built like a mansion. A well-ordered family mansion. Everything so vertical. No lurking danger, no flaw in the oneness of this vision, in the
30 oneness of a landscape within which he is safely lodged.

- Look at how texts are structured and presented in order to influence the reader's point of view
- Understand the meaning and effect of new and unfamiliar words
- Investigate the origin of words

Word origins

aviator (n), from the French word *aviateur*, meaning 'pilot'. This, in turn, comes from the Latin word *avis*, meaning 'bird'. Early in the history of flying, 'aviator' was used to distinguish a pilot from an aeronaut (a balloonist).

Related words:
- aviation
- avian

starboard (n), from the Old English word *steorbord*, meaning the 'side on which a vessel is steered' (*stear* means 'rudder' or 'steering paddle' and *bord* means 'ship's side').

sabotage (n), from the French verb *saboter*, meaning 'to attempt deliberately to make a plan or action fail'.

Related word:
- saboteur

Glossary

altitude height of something
recumbent lying down, reclining
torrent strong or fast-moving water
acceleration rate at which the speed of something increases
quiver tremble or shake
rudimentary elementary, not fully developed

Flying into a storm

"Time to leave. Good-bye." And Bernis takes off again.

He plunges into a storm, which batters at the plane like the pick-axe of a wrecker. He's been through others, he'll come through this one too. Bernis's thoughts are rudimentary, thoughts

5 geared to action: how to climb out of this ring of mountains into which the whirling down-draughts are sucking him, how to see through this diluvial night and jump the black wall of whipping rain, and come out on to the sea?

A sudden shudder! Has something snapped? Suddenly the

10 plane lurches towards the left. Bernis holds it back with one, then two hands, and then with every sinew of his body. [...] The plane drops earthwards like a weight. Bernis is done for. One more second and he'll be flung forever from that suddenly troubled mansion he was just beginning to understand. Fields,

15 forests, villages will spiral up towards him. The smoke of appearances, wraiths of smoke, smoke! And here's a sheepfold doing somersaults across the sky. [...]

"Phew! A nasty fright!" A kick to the rudder-paddle frees a cable. A jammed control? Sabotage? No. Nothing. Nothing at

20 all. A simple kick of the heel re-establishes the world. But what a close thing!

From *Southern Mail* by Antoine de Saint-Exupéry

Phew! That was close!

Now it's your turn to write a short piece about a dramatic experience.

- Imagine a scenario in which something suddenly goes drastically wrong.
- Make use of literary devices such as metaphor, simile, onomatopoeia, alliteration and internal speech to enhance your writing.
- Consider the scene, setting and point of view you will write from (first- or third-person).

When you have finished, swap your writing with a partner and comment on each other's work.

> **Language tip**
> **Onomatopoeia** is a literary device in which a word sounds similar to the noise it is describing. Here are some examples from the extract on this page: 'whip', 'snap'.

- Explain how an author develops character, setting and plot
- Choose a viewpoint to write from
- Use literary and rhetorical devices to enhance the impact of writing

Comprehension

1 Looking at the first extract, compare Bernis's feelings and sensations while landing the plane with being back on the ground.

2 What happens in the second extract to cause the sudden and quick descent of the plane? What happens next?

3 What is 'sabotage'? What does Bernis think might have been done?

1 Choose two metaphors or similes in the first extract and explain why you find them particularly effective.

2 In the second extract, why do you think the writer uses Bernis's internal monologue to communicate his thoughts?

1 How does this account compare with other stories of adventure and survival that you have read?

2 Would you take such risks yourself?

131

A kite-fighting tournament

The following extract is from *The Kite Runner*, a novel set in Afghanistan in the 1970s. The author, Khaled Hosseini, was born in Afghanistan and lived there until 1980, when he and his family were granted asylum in America. He is now a doctor in California.

Amir and Hassan are 12-year-old boys who love the local kite-fighting tournament. The two boys are close friends, but it is Hassan who excels as a kite runner.

Hassan

It quickly became apparent that Hassan and I were better kite fighters than kite makers. Some flaw or other in our design always ruined them. So Baba started taking us to
5 Saifo's to buy our kites. Saifo was a nearly blind old man who was a *mochi* by profession – a shoe repairman. But he was also the city's most famous kite maker, working out of a tiny hovel on Jedeh Maywand, the crowded street south
10 of the muddy banks of the Kabul River. I remember you had to crouch to enter the tiny store, and then had to lift a trapdoor to creep down a set of wooden steps to the dank basement where Saifo stored his coveted kites. Baba would buy us each three identical kites and spools of glass string.

15 The kite fighting tournament was an old winter tradition in Afghanistan. It started early in the morning on the day of the contest and didn't end until only the winning kite flew in the sky. People gathered on sidewalks and roofs to cheer for their kids. The streets filled with kite fighters, jerking and tugging
20 on their lines, squinting up to the sky, trying to gain position to cut the opponent's line. [...] The real fun began when a kite was cut. That was where the kite runners came in, those kids who chased the wind-blown kite drifting through their neighbourhoods until it came spiralling down in a field, dropping
25 in someone's yard, on a tree, or a rooftop. The chase got pretty fierce; hordes of kite runners swarmed the streets, shoved past each other like those people in Spain I'd read about once who ran from bulls. [...]

Thousands of children prepare to set a new world record for the number of kites flown simultaneously on 30 July 2009.

Glossary

hovel small, badly built house
dank unpleasantly cold or chilly
horde large group or crowd

- Evaluate how writers develop ideas and themes in their writing
- Find evidence in a text about the environment, culture and social situation

30 For kite runners, the most coveted prize was the last fallen kite of a winter tournament. It was a trophy of honour, something to be displayed for guests to admire. When the sky cleared of kites and only the final two remained, every kite runner got ready for the chance to land this prize. He positioned himself at a spot that he thought would give him a head start. Tense

35 muscles ready to uncoil. Necks craned. Eyes crinkled. Fights broke out. And when the last kite was cut, all hell broke loose.

Over the years I had seen a lot of kids run kites. But Hassan was by far the greatest runner I'd ever seen. It was downright eerie the way he always got to the spot the kite would land

40 before the kite did, as if he had some sort of inner compass. I remember one overcast winter day, Hassan and I were running a kite. I was chasing him through neighbourhoods, hopping gutters, weaving through narrow streets. I was a year older than him, but Hassan ran faster than I did, and I was falling behind.

45 "Hassan! Wait!" I yelled, my breathing hot and ragged.

He whirled round, motioned with his hand. "This way!" he called before dashing around another corner. I looked up, saw that the direction in which we were running was opposite to the one in which the kite was drifting.

50 "We're losing it! We're going the wrong way!" I cried out.

"Trust me!" I heard him call up ahead.

I reached the corner and saw Hassan bolting along, his head down, not even looking at the sky, sweat soaking through the back of his shirt. I tripped over a rock and fell – I wasn't just

55 slower than Hassan but clumsier, too; I'd always envied his natural athleticism. When I staggered to my feet, I caught a glimpse of Hassan disappearing around another street corner. I hobbled after him, in pain because of my scraped knees.

I saw we had ended up on a rutted dirt road near Isteqlal

60 Middle School. There was a field on one side where lettuce grew in the summer, and a row of sour cherry trees on the other. I found Hassan sitting cross-legged at the foot of one of the trees, eating from a fistful of dried mulberries.

"What are we doing here?" I panted, feeling sick in the stomach.

Glossary

covet wish for something that belongs to another
uncoil straighten from a coiled or curled position
eerie strange and mysterious
plummet drop downwards quickly

- Evaluate how writers develop ideas and themes in their writing
- Find evidence in a text about the environment, culture and social situation
- Understand how a point of view is conveyed in a text
- Participate fully in discussions

65 He smiled. "Sit with me, Amir."

I dropped next to him, lay on a thin patch of snow, wheezing. "You're wasting our time. It was going the other way, didn't you see?"

Hassan popped a mulberry in his mouth. "It's coming," he said.
70 I could hardly breathe and he didn't even seem tired.

"How do you know?" I said.

"I know."

"How can you *know*?"

He turned to me. A few sweat beads rolled from his bald scalp.
75 "Would I ever lie to you, Amir?" he said, and then suddenly pointing to the sky, "Here it comes!" He rose to his feet and walked a few paces to his left. I looked up, saw the kite plummeting towards us. I heard footfalls, shouts, an approaching crowd of kite runners. But they were wasting their time. Because
80 Hassan stood with his arms wide open, smiling, waiting for the kite.

From *The Kite Runner* by KHALED HOSSEINI

Glossary

mulberry purple or white fruit (similar to a blackberry)

Comprehension

1 Why did Amir's father take the boys to the kite store?

2 What was the ultimate trophy for a kite runner?

3 Compare the physical abilities of Hassan and Amir.

1 Make a list of all the verbs used to drive the action of the story. Then:
   a Look up the definitions of those you are less familiar with.
   b Compose your own sentence using your unfamiliar verbs.

2 How does the writer use language and sentence structure to build tension and excitement in lines 31–36?

1 How does this story convey Amir's respect and admiration for his friend Hassan?

2 What does it reveal about the differences between them?

3 What does this story demonstrate about the importance in relationships of sharing and trust?

9 Cities

What is so special about cities?

Talk about ...

- Discuss the cities you know best.
- What is the oldest city you have ever visited, and what is life like there today?
- How should we plan to create more sustainable cities for the future?

> **Look 'round thee now on Samarcand!**
> **Is she not queen of Earth? her pride**
> **Above all cities? in her hand**
> **Their destinies?**
>
> From 'Tamerlane' by EDGAR ALLAN POE

Seri Wawasan Bridge, Putrajaya, Malaysia

Do you know where Samarkand is? One of the oldest cities in the world, it was once part of Persia (modern-day Iran) and is now in Uzbekistan. You can see a picture of it above. In its heyday, up to the fourteenth century, it was a major city on the old Silk Road – the trade route between China and Western Europe that runs all the way to the Mediterranean Sea.

By contrast, the city of Putrajaya, in Malaysia, is one of the world's newer cities. Established almost 9,000 years after Samarkand, in 1995, the city was made Malaysia's new administrative centre with a focus on sustainability and modern technological features.

What are the top cities of the world?

We have reached a point in history where more people live in cities than in small towns and rural communities. What do you think are the biggest cities in the world today in terms of population? If you had made your top ten list in 1950, do you think your list would have been the same?

Now look at the population data charts below. Are there any surprises?

- Undertake research and prepare detailed notes for writing and presentations
- Participate fully in discussions
- Write a range of non-fiction texts

The ten largest cities in 2022

1	Tokyo, Japan	37,435,191
2	Delhi, India	29,399,141
3	Shanghai, China	26,317,104
4	São Paulo, Brazil	21,846,507
5	Mexico City, Mexico	21,671,908
6	Cairo, Egypt	20,484,965
7	Dhaka, Bangladesh	20,283,552
8	Mumbai, India	20,185,064
9	Beijing, China	20,035,455
10	Osaka, Japan	19,222,665

The ten largest cities in 1950

1	New York, USA	12,340,000
2	Tokyo, Japan	11,270,000
3	London, UK	8,346,000
4	Osaka, Japan	7,010,000
5	Paris, France	6,280,000
6	Moscow, Russia	5,360,000
7	Buenos Aires, Argentina	5,170,000
8	Kolkata, India	4,600,000
9	Shanghai, China	4,290,000
10	Chicago, USA	3,621,000

The ten largest cities in 1500

1	Beijing, China	672,000
2	Vijayanagar, India	500,000
3	Cairo, Egypt	400,000
4	Hangzhou, China	250,000
5	Tabriz, Iran	250,000
6	Constantinople (Istanbul), Turkey	200,000
7	Gauḍa, India	200,000
8	Paris, France	185,000
9	Guangzhou, China	150,000
10	Nanjing, China	147,000

The ten largest cities in 1000

1	Córdoba, Spain	450,000
2	Kaifeng, China	400,000
3	Constantinople (Istanbul), Turkey	300,000
4	Angkor, Cambodia	200,000
5	Kyoto, Japan	175,000
6	Cairo, Egypt	135,000
7	Baghdad, Iraq	125,000
8	Nishapur (Neyshabur), Iran	125,000
9	Al-Hasa, Saudi Arabia	110,000
10	Patan (Anhilwara), India	100,000

Analyzing the data

Write a paragraph in answer to each of the questions below.

- Looking at the charts, what can you deduce about how the world has changed since 1950?
- What happens when we go back to earlier centuries?
- What is the effect of the growth of megacities? These are cities of more then 10 million people.

Talk about ...

- Can you locate these cities on a world map?
- What do these charts tell you about our changing world?
- What do you think the population of Tokyo might be in another 50 years?

An essayist's concept of 'Town'

In the essay 'Town', the English writer Holbrook Jackson is making a general point rather than writing about a specific town, city or country. Below is an extract from the essay, first published in 1913.

- Think about how writers use themes and conventions in a range of poetic forms to achieve a particular effect
- Understand how point of view is conveyed in a text
- Investigate the origin of words

Town

When I write of Town, not of this town or that town, not of London or Paris, neither of Venice, nor Oxford, nor Florence, nor Bruges, nor Rome; nor yet write I of Bagdad or Babylon, Damascus or Samarkand. I write of Town.
5   I celebrate all of these great cities in the soul of each – domed or towered or turreted, roofed in red or grey or purple, walled or free, filled with trees or threaded by river or canal, piercing heaven with spire or striking it with minaret – it is all of these in the final expression of man's
10   creativeness – Town.

HOLBROOK JACKSON

Language tip
'Neither' and 'nor' are conjunctions that connect two or more negative alternatives.

'Nor' usually follows 'neither' when they're used in the same sentence:

'She likes neither apples nor bananas.'

Comprehension

A

1 Why does the writer focus on domes, turrets, towers and roofs in this essay?
2 In what way is Jackson's idea of 'Town' different to the 'great cities' he mentions by name?

B

1 What effect is created by the writer's repetition of 'I write'?
2 What is the significance of the repeated use of the conjunctions 'neither' and 'nor'?
3 Write two example sentences about cities or towns of your own using 'neither' and 'nor'.

C

1 What other points do you think Jackson may go on to make in the rest of the essay?
2 Together, plan and write a short piece about where you live in the style of 'Town'. Include some of your ideas from the previous question.

Talk about ...
- What is your idea of an ideal city or town?
- And what would be its opposite?

Word origins

town (n), from the Old English *tūn*, meaning 'an enclosed piece of land, a homestead or village'
city (n), from the Old French *cité*, and Latin *civitas*, meaning 'citizenship'
Related words:
- citizen
- citizenship

A view from the window in San Francisco

The following extract from the novel *McTeague: A Story of San Francisco* by Frank Norris was published in 1899. It describes the life of a man known as McTeague (whose first name is never revealed). McTeague opens a dentist shop which he calls a 'parlor' on Polk Street in the neighbourhood of Polk Gulch, where he lives and works. Much of his time is spent observing the view from the window.

Since 1873, cable cars have served the hilly terrain of San Francisco. At the time Norris was writing, they were powered by steam engines and each cable car line had its own powerhouse.

Cable cars in San Francisco in the late nineteenth/early twentieth centuries

Polk Street, San Francisco

The street never failed to interest him. It woke to its work about seven o'clock, at the time when the newsboys made their appearance together with the day laborers. The laborers went trudging past in a straggling
5 file – plumbers' apprentices, their pockets stuffed with sections of lead pipe, tweezers, and pliers; carpenters, carrying nothing but their little lunch baskets; gangs of street workers, their overalls soiled with yellow clay, their picks and long-handled shovels over their shoulders; plasterers, spotted with lime from
10 head to foot. This little army of workers, tramping steadily in one direction, met and mingled with other workers of a different description – conductors and 'swing men' of the cable company going on duty; heavy-eyed night clerks from the pharmacies on their way home to sleep; police officers returning to the
15 police station to make their night report, and Chinese market gardeners teetering past under their heavy baskets. The cable cars began to fill up; all along the street could be seen the shopkeepers taking down their shutters.

Between seven and eight the street breakfasted. Now and then
20 a waiter from one of the cheap restaurants crossed from one sidewalk to the other, balancing on one palm a tray covered with a napkin. Everywhere was the smell of coffee and of frying meat. A little later, following in the path of the day laborers, came the clerks and shop girls, dressed with a certain cheap
25 smartness, always in a hurry, glancing apprehensively at the powerhouse clock. Their employers followed an hour or so later – on the cable cars for the most part whiskered gentlemen

Glossary

trudging walking slowly and wearily

lime white, chalky substance used to make whitewash for painting walls and ceilings

apprehensively anxiously

stragglers people who are left behind from the main group

impromptu without any planning or preparation

vantage point place from which you have a good view of something

- Explain how an author develops characters, setting and plot

with huge stomachs, reading the morning papers with great gravity; bank cashiers and insurance clerks with flowers in their buttonholes.

At the same time the schoolchildren invaded the street, filling the air with a clamor of shrill voices, stopping at the stationers' shops, or idling a moment in the doorways of the candy stores. For over half an hour they held possession of the sidewalks, then suddenly disappeared, leaving behind one or two stragglers who hurried along with great strides of their little thin legs, very anxious and preoccupied.

Towards eleven o'clock the ladies from the great avenue a block above Polk Street made their appearance, promenading the sidewalks leisurely, deliberately. They were at their morning's marketing. They were handsome women, beautifully dressed. They knew by name their butchers and grocers and vegetable men. From his window McTeague saw them in front of the stalls, gloved and veiled. They all seemed to know one another, these grand ladies from the fashionable avenue. Meetings took place here and there; a conversation was begun; others arrived; groups were formed; little impromptu meetings were held before the chopping blocks of butchers' stalls, or on the sidewalk, around boxes of berries and fruit.

From noon to evening the population of the street was of a mixed character. The street was busiest at that time; a vast and prolonged murmur arose – the mingled shuffling of feet, the rattle of wheels, the heavy trundling of cable cars. At four o'clock the school children once more swarmed the sidewalks, again disappearing with surprising suddenness. At six the great homeward march commenced; the cars were crowded, the laborers thronged the sidewalks, the newsboys chanted the evening papers. Then all at once the street fell quiet; hardly a soul was in sight; the sidewalks were deserted. It was supper hour. Evening began; and one by one a multitude of lights grew thick from street corner to street corner. Once more the street was crowded. Now there was no thought but for amusement. The cable cars were loaded with theatre-goers – men in high hats and young girls in furred opera cloaks. On the sidewalks were groups

Talk about ...
- Do people have more freedom to choose their own working hours now than they did back in 1900?
- What are the defining characteristics of daily life in cities today?
- How have people's lives and lifestyles changed since this novel was written?

Labourer in San Francisco watching the world go by

• Examine closely how texts mirror the time and place in which they are written
• Explain how an author develops characters, setting and plot
• Explain how language features create effect

and couples – the plumbers' apprentices, the girls of the ribbon counters, the little families that lived on the second stories over
70 their shops, the dressmakers, the small doctors, the harness-makers – all the various inhabitants of the street were abroad, strolling idly from shop window to shop window, taking the air after the day's work.

Then, little by little, Polk Street dropped back to solitude. Eleven
75 o'clock struck from the powerhouse clock. Lights were extinguished. At one o'clock the cable stopped, leaving an abrupt silence in the air. All at once it seemed very still. The ugly noises were the occasional footfalls of a policeman and the persistent calling of ducks and geese in the closed market. The street was asleep.

80 Day after day, McTeague saw the same panorama unroll itself. The bay window of his 'Dental Parlors' was for him a vantage point from which he watched the world go past.

From *McTeague: A Story of San Francisco* by FRANK NORRIS

Why do people like to watch the world go by?

Stretch zone

Write about your window view of the city. It could be the view as seen from your window at school or at home – or, perhaps, from a bus, a car or a train travelling through the city on your way somewhere.

Comprehension

1 What types of buildings and services described here are what you might expect to find in a typical large town or city of around 1900 in the United States?

2 List all the examples of jobs and occupations that are mentioned in the extract.

3 How is the dress and behaviour of the women described? Find examples from the text and explain them in context.

4 What essential services of the city are shut down at night to put the street to sleep?

1 Explain the following phrases in more modern language:
  a 'idling a moment' (line 33)
  b 'promenading the sidewalks' (lines 39–40)
  c 'no thought but for amusement' (lines 64–65)

1 Do you think this text is meant to be a satire or an accurate portrayal of the way people in San Francisco lived around 1900?

2 How typical is this portrait of a day in the life of a city? Discuss with your partner or group and compare it with other cities that you know of.

Life in a street in Paris

Paris has often featured in great novels of the nineteenth and twentieth centuries. In this semi-autobiographical account by the British writer George Orwell, published in 1933, he describes city life from the point of view of its poorest inhabitants. It starts out with a description of life in a boarding house in Paris.

- Consider the influence of literature from different historical periods
- Find evidence in a text about the environment, culture and social situation

Street scene in Paris, painted in 1926 by Christopher Wood

Language tip
Personification is a literary device that gives human characteristics to non-human things, such as animals, plants, ideas, the weather, or inanimate objects. It can add vivid imagery, feeling and atmosphere to a text.

For example:

'The wind howled through the trees.'

'The old bench groaned as they all sat down.'

The rue du Coq d'Or, Paris

The rue du Coq d'Or, Paris, seven in the morning. A succession of furious, choking yells from the street. Madame Monce, who kept the little hotel opposite mine, had come out on to the pavement to address a lodger on the third floor. Her bare feet were stuck into sabots and her grey hair was streaming down.

Madame Monce: "How many times have I told you not to squash bugs on the wallpaper? Do you think you've bought

Glossary

sabot wooden shoe made of a single piece of wood shaped and hollowed out to fit the foot

cavalry soldiers who fight on horseback

hawker someone who sells goods in the street

navvy (plural 'navvies') labourer employed in the construction of a canal, road or railway

- Read literature from different historical periods, and discuss the influence on literature today
- Understand how a point of view is conveyed in a text
- Use inference and deduction to identify evidence about the environment, culture and social situation
- Examine how a writer's use of language and grammatical features creates effect and meaning

the hotel, eh? Why can't you throw them out of the window like everyone else?"

10 Thereupon a chorus of yells, as windows were flung open on every side and half the street joined in the quarrel. They shut up abruptly ten minutes later, when a squadron of cavalry rode past and people stopped shouting to look at them.

I sketch this scene, just to convey something of the spirit of the
15 rue du Coq d'Or. Not that quarrels were the only thing that happened there – but still, we seldom got through the morning without at least one outburst of this description. Quarrels, and the desolate cries of street hawkers, and the shouts of children chasing orange-peel over the cobbles, and at
20 night loud singing and the sour reek of the refuse-carts, made up the atmosphere of the street.

It was a very narrow street – a ravine of tall, leprous houses, lurching towards one another
25 in queer attitudes, as though they had all been frozen in the act of collapse. All the houses were hotels and packed to the tiles with lodgers. [...] At the foot of the hotels were tiny bistros.

On Saturday nights there was fighting, and
30 the navvies who lived in the cheapest hotels used to conduct mysterious feuds, and fight them out with chairs and occasionally revolvers. At night the policemen would only come through the street two together. It was a fairly
35 rackety place. And yet amid the noise and dirt lived the usual respectable French shopkeepers, bakers and laundresses and the like, keeping themselves to themselves and quietly piling up small fortunes. It was quite a representative
40 Paris slum.

From *Down and Out in Paris and London* by
GEORGE ORWELL

Comprehension

A

1 What does being 'down and out' mean?
2 How do we know that this is a very crowded part of Paris?
3 Why do you think the people who live here quarrel so much?
4 Why do you think the police liked to patrol this part of the city in groups of two?

B

1 What technique does the writer use to describe the houses in lines 23–26?
2 What effect does this create?
3 List the words and phrases which describe or imply:
   a a very noisy neighbourhood
   b bad behaviour and conflict
   c dirt, insect infestations and rubbish

C

1 Describe the overall mood and tone of this extract, and what you think the author's intention was in writing it.

Istanbul's wooden mansions

The writer Orhan Pamuk has lived all his life in Istanbul and has a great affection for the city that is also the source of his earliest memories of childhood. He calls his family home a 'museum house' because of the large formal sitting room where he was not allowed to play. In this room, the curtains were permanently drawn in order to protect the old photographs and objects from the heat, light and dust.

- Evaluate how writers develop ideas and themes in their writing
- Discuss the meaning of new and unfamiliar words

Black and white

Accustomed as I was to the semi-darkness of our bleak museum house, I preferred being indoors. The street below, the avenues beyond, the city's poor neighbourhoods seemed as dangerous as those in a black-and-white gangster film. And with this
5 attraction to the shadow world, I have always preferred the winter to the summer in Istanbul. I love the early evenings when autumn is slipping into winter, when the leafless trees are trembling in the north wind and people in black coats and jackets are rushing home through the darkening streets. I love
10 the overwhelming melancholy when I look at the walls of old apartment buildings and the dark surfaces of neglected, unpainted, fallen-down wooden mansions: only in Istanbul have I seen this texture, this shading. When I watch the black-and-white crowds rushing through the darkening streets on a
15 winter evening, I feel a deep sense of fellowship, almost as if the night has cloaked our lives, our streets, our every belonging in a blanket of darkness, as if once we're safe in our houses, our bedrooms, our beds, we can return to dreams of our long-gone riches, our legendary past.

20 The wooden mansions of my childhood, and the smaller, more modest wooden houses in the city's back streets, were in a mesmerizing state of ruin. Poverty and neglect had ensured these houses were never painted, and the combination of age, dirt and humidity slowly darkened the wood to give that
25 special colour, that unique texture, so prevalent in the back-street neighbourhood I saw as a child that I took the blackness to be original. Some houses had a brown under-tone, and perhaps there were those in the poorest streets that had never known paint.

Istanbul, Old Town

Glossary

gangster member of a gang of criminals
melancholy feeling of thoughtful sadness

143

- Understand how a point of view is conveyed in a text
- Read a variety of texts and evaluate how writers develop ideas and themes in their writing

30 In the summer, when these old wooden houses would dry out, turn a dark, chalky, tinderbox brown, you could imagine them catching fire at any moment. During the winter's long cold spells, the snow and the rain endowed these same houses with the mildew hint of rotting wood. So it was too with the old

35 wooden lodges, now mostly abandoned and of interest only to street urchins, ghosts and antique hunters. They would awaken in me the same degrees of fear, worry and curiosity; as I peered at them over the half-broken walls through the damp trees and into the broken windows, a chill would pass

40 through me.

From *Istanbul: Memories of a City* by ORHAN PAMUK

Glossary

endowed gave/provided
mildew type of fungus which grows in damp places

Comprehension

A

1 What reason does the writer give for preferring to view his city in shadows and half-light?

2 What causes the writer to feel a sense of melancholy?

3 How is Istanbul's old city slowly disappearing, and what is the writer's response to this?

B

1 Analyze the descriptions provided of the old buildings of Istanbul. List the:

  a different types of residential buildings and what has happened to them

  b colour terms and textures that are the 'special colour' of Istanbul's old houses

2 Reread lines 20–29. Find the positive phrases the writer uses to describe aspects of decay and ruin in the city.

3 Replace the positive adjectives with negative ones to see how this changes the overall feeling of the extract.

C

1 Decide how you could represent these descriptions for a graphic presentation through sketching, drawing or digitally reproducing them.

2 Put your visuals together with the descriptions and share with other pairs.

A portrait of Venice

Venice is one of the best-preserved old cities in Europe, and is like a living work of art, with its elegant *palazzi* ('palaces' in Italian) and canals that are the transport routes of the city.

Venice is famous for its opera, art and carnival (where people dress up in historical costumes and wear masks). John Berendt writes about his experience of getting to know the Venetian people behind the mask in the late 1990s.

View of the Grand Canal from the South, the Palazzo Foscari to the right and the Rialto Bridge beyond, painted by Giovanni Antonio Canal (Canaletto) in the eighteenth century

The Venice effect

"Everyone in Venice is acting," Count Girolama Marcello told me. "Everyone plays a role, and the role changes. The key to understanding Venetians is rhythm – the rhythm of the lagoons, the rhythm of the water, the tides, the waves." [...]

5   I had been walking along Calle della Mandola when I ran into Count Marcello. He was a member of an old Venetian family and was considered an authority on the history, the social structure, and especially the subtleties of Venice. As we were both headed in the same direction, I joined him.

10 "The rhythm in Venice is like breathing," he said. "High water, high pressure: tense. Low water, low pressure: relaxed. Venetians are not at all attuned to the rhythm of the wheel. That is for other places, places with motor vehicles. Ours is the rhythm of the Adriatic. The rhythm of the sea. In Venice the rhythm
15 flows along with the tide, and the tide changes every six hours."

Talk about ...
- Discuss the differences between the 'rhythm of the wheel' and the 'rhythm of the sea'.
- Which rhythm would you prefer to live by?

- Understand how a point of view is conveyed in a text
- Read a variety of texts and evaluate how writers develop ideas and themes in their writing

Count Marcello inhaled deeply. "How do you see a bridge?"

"Pardon me?" I asked. "A bridge?"

"Do you see a bridge as an obstacle – as just another set of steps to climb to get from one side of the canal to the other?
20 We Venetians do not see bridges as obstacles. To us bridges are transitions. We go over them very slowly. They are part of the rhythm. They are the links between two parts of a theatre, like changes in scenery, or like the progression from Act One of a play to Act Two. Our role changes as we go over bridges.
25 We cross from one reality … to another reality. From one street … to another street. From one setting … to another setting."

We were approaching a bridge crossing over Rio di San Luca into Campo Manin.

30 "A *trompe l'œil* painting," Count Marcello went on, "is a painting that is so lifelike it doesn't look like a painting at all. It looks like real life, but of course it is not. It is reality once removed. What, then, is a *trompe l'œil* painting when it is reflected in a mirror? Reality twice removed?

35 "Sunlight on a canal is reflected up through a window on to the ceiling, then from the ceiling on to a vase, and from the vase on to a glass, or a silver bowl. Which is the real sunlight? Which is the real reflection? What is true? What is not true? The answer is not so simple, because the truth can change. I can change. You
40 can change. That is the Venice effect."

Glossary

trompe l'œil in French means 'deceives the eye' – the term is used to describe a painting that tricks you into thinking the painted scene is real

We descended from the bridge into Campo Manin. Other than having come from the deep shade of Calle della Mandola into the bright sunlight of the open square, I felt unchanged. My role, whatever it was, remained the same as it had been before
45 the bridge. I did not of course admit this to Count Marcello. But I looked at him to see if he would acknowledge having undergone any change himself.

He breathed deeply as we walked into Campo Manin. Then, with an air of finality, he said, "Venetians never tell the truth.
50 We mean precisely the opposite of what we say."

From *The City of Falling Angels* by JOHN BERENDT

- Read a variety of texts and evaluate how writers develop ideas and themes in their writing

Comprehension

1 Where do the Venetians get their special sense of rhythm from, according to Count Marcello?

2 What does the Count mean by the less-useful 'rhythm of the wheel' in Venetian society?

3 What role do the bridges of Venice play, apart from providing a way to cross the canals?

4 List all the features of Venice described in this extract that relate to the visual, literary or performing arts.

B

1 Look at line 10. How effective is the simile of the rhythm of Venice being like 'breathing'?

2 How does the illusion and the metaphor of a *trompe l'œil* painting contribute to our understanding of 'the Venice effect'?

C

1 If according to Count Marcello, "Everyone in Venice is acting" (line 1), does this mean that the city itself becomes a stage or theatre?

2 Come up with a definition of the 'Venice effect' in your own words, and think of how it might apply to other cities and social contexts.

Writing the city

Write your own account of a city that you love or would like to know more about.

- Do some background research into the history, the people, the industries and the events that have made your chosen city what it is today.
- Focus on aspects of the city that capture its everyday feel, and not just the historical landmarks and tourist hotspots.
- Draw on representations of your city in literature, art, photography, film and TV.
- Decide on the purpose of your writing – is it a promotional feature, an entry in Wikipedia, or a professional or personal viewpoint?
- Put yourself in the picture. What are you doing there, and who are you with? What is happening right now?
- Include photographs and sketches to support your account (it might be easier to present as a digital file or presentation).
- Share your account with other members of your group, and exchange feedback on each other's city accounts.

- Carry out comprehensive research using a range of sources
- Select the most appropriate forms for media and multimedia elements in a presentation
- Adapt writing style and register for intended audience and purpose

Tokyo, Japan: the bright lights of Akihabara

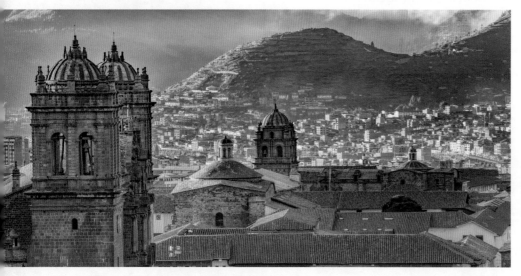

Cusco, Peru: morning sun on the Plaza de Armas

Stretch zone

What are the future predictions around population growth in your chosen city? Research strategies to make your chosen city more sustainable and prepared for the impacts of climate change.

Paris, France: still from the television programme *Emily in Paris*

10 Making a difference

How can we all help change the world for the better?

Success isn't about how much money you make, it's about the difference you make in people's lives.

MICHELLE OBAMA

Talk about ...

- Who do you most admire? What makes them so remarkable?

- Come up with your own top ten public figures and explain why you rate them so highly.

- Do you find it motivating to read about the lives of famous and not-so-famous achievers?

In one way or another we all want to make a difference, to contribute in some small way to something bigger than ourselves. Doing what you believe in and are good at is also more likely to make you happy and successful in life.

Is there anyone you know, or have read about, that you consider to be a role model?

They might not be famous, but could be well-known to those working in their chosen field or appreciated by their community for what they contribute.

149

- Find evidence in a text about the environment, culture and social situation
- Understand how point of view is conveyed in a text
- Participate fully in discussions

An inspirational climate campaigner

When 15-year-old Greta Thunberg decided to go on strike and protest outside the Swedish parliament in order to condemn and influence her country's policies on climate change, she was doing what she felt she needed to do. Her parents and her teachers were at first reluctant to support her taking weeks off school, but they eventually supported Greta and her cause. Greta's cause ended up sparking a global movement for action against the climate crisis, inspiring millions of school students to go on strike for the planet. Some people, however, are in opposition to strikes and protests, especially when they involve children and missing school.

The following speech was made at the United Nations Climate Change Conference in Katowice, Poland, in December 2018.

Unpopular

My name is Greta Thunberg, I am fifteen years old and I'm from Sweden. I speak on behalf of Climate Justice Now.

Many people say that Sweden is just a small country and it doesn't matter what we do. But I've learnt that no one is too
5 small to make a difference. And if a few children can get headlines all over the world just by not going to school – then imagine what we all could do together if we really wanted to.

But to do that we have to speak clearly. No matter how uncomfortable that may be. You only speak of green, eternal
10 economic growth because you are all too scared of being unpopular. You only talk about moving forward with the same bad ideas that got us into this mess. Even when the only sensible thing to do is to pull the emergency brake.

You are not mature enough to tell it like it is. Even that burden
15 you leave to your children. But I don't care about being popular, I care about climate justice and the living planet.

We are about to sacrifice our civilization for the opportunity of a very small number of people to continue to make enormous amounts of money. We are about to sacrifice the biosphere so
20 that rich people in countries like mine can live in luxury. But it is the sufferings of the many which pay for the luxuries of the few.

The year 2078 I will celebrate my seventy-fifth birthday. If I have children, then maybe they will spend that day with me.

?

Why is it good to take a stand even if you risk being unpopular?

25 Maybe they will ask about you. Maybe they will ask why you didn't do anything, while there still was time to act. You say that you love your children above everything else. And yet you are stealing their future in front of their very eyes.

Until you start focusing on what needs to be done rather than what is politically possible, there's no hope. We cannot solve
30 a crisis. We need to keep the fossil fuels in the ground and we need to focus on equity.

And if solutions within this system are so impossible to find then maybe we should change the system itself?

We have not come here to beg world leaders to care. You have
35 ignored us in the past and you will ignore us again. You've run out of excuses and we're running out of time. We've come here to let you know that change is coming whether you like it or not.

The real power belongs to the people. Thank you.

Word origins

civilization (n), comes from the Latin word *civilis*, meaning 'civil', or 'to do with city or citizens' life'

biosphere (n), comes from the Greek *bios*, meaning one's 'life, lifetime or way of living', and *sphaira*, meaning a 'ball' or 'globe'
Related words:
- biology

equity (n), comes from the Latin word *aequus*, meaning 'equal' or 'just'
Related words:
- equal
- equality
- equivalent
- equanimous

Comprehension

A

1 How does Greta Thunberg make the best of being small and a young person in an adult world? Support your answer with examples from the text.

2 List the key points in the speech that highlight Thunberg's view that the current political and economic system is failing the planet.

3 Which two things does she say need to be done?

B

1 What does the metaphor of the 'emergency brake' suggest to you?

2 a Who is Thunberg referring to when she uses the first-person plural ('we' and 'us')?

   b Who is she addressing when she uses the second person?

3 Find examples of repetition in the extract and explain how Thunberg's use of this technique enhances her speech.

C

1 What difference do you think Thunberg's actions have made in drawing world attention to the climate crisis and other social issues?

What do you feel strongly about?

Write a speech on a topic that matters to you. Decide on where and when you will present it, and how your speech responds to your time and place in the world.

- Do some research to support your cause or topic and show how you try to address these challenges in your own life. Think of ways that you can connect the local with global issues.
- Remember, you are writing a speech that people will hear, so keep it short, conversational and upbeat in tone.
- Read through the speech writing tips in the box on the right. Make sure you try to include as many of them as possible in your writing.

Now present your speech to your partner or group. You can also practise by recording it on a computer or phone so that you can listen back to yourself later.

- Carry out comprehensive research on a range of topics
- Make sure text type, structure and style are suitable for intended audience
- Participate in group discussions and debates

Speech writing tips

1. Introduce yourself.
2. Make an engaging opening statement.
3. Do the research to support your argument.
4. Use persuasive language to engage your audience.
5. Add a surprise statement or personal insight.
6. Use a famous quote or example from history.
7. Keep it short and focused on one or two clear ideas.
8. Think of a motivating point to end on.

?

Imagine two scenarios 50 years in the future. One is where world leaders have acted on Greta Thunberg's climate and social equality warnings, and the other is where they haven't. Discuss how everyday life might be for you in each scenario. Which one do you prefer?

Popular science

First published in 1962, Rachel Carson's *Silent Spring* described the harmful effects of pesticides on the environment, leading to the banning of the insecticide DDT in most countries. The book helped launch the environmental movement in the United States.

The following extract is the first chapter in the book, and it shows how the writer combined scientific knowledge with poetic writing to get her message across.

- Examine and discuss a wide range of texts
- Look at how texts are structured and presented in order to influence the reader's point of view

A fable for tomorrow

There was once a town in the heart of America where all life seemed to live in harmony with its surroundings. The town lay in the midst of a
5   checkerboard of prosperous farms, with fields of grain and hillsides of orchards where, in spring, white clouds of bloom drifted above the green fields. In autumn, oak and maple
10 and birch set up a blaze of colour that flamed and flickered across a backdrop of pines. Then foxes barked in the hills and deer silently crossed the fields, half hidden in the mists of the fall mornings.
15

Along the roads, laurel, viburnum and alder, great ferns and wildflowers delighted the traveller's eye through much of the year. Even in winter the roadsides were places of beauty, where countless birds came to feed on the berries and on the seed heads of the dried weeds rising above the snow. The countryside
20 was, in fact, famous for the abundance and variety of its bird life, and when the flood of migrants was pouring through in spring and autumn people travelled from great distances to observe them. Others came to fish the streams, which flowed clear and cold out of the hills and contained shady pools where
25 trout lay. So it had been from the days many years ago when the first settlers raised their houses, sank their wells, and built their barns.

- Examine and discuss a wide range of texts
- Look at how texts are structured and presented in order to influence the reader's point of view
- Understand the meaning and effect of new and unfamiliar words

30 Then a strange blight crept over the area and everything began to change. Some evil spell had settled on the community: mysterious maladies swept the flocks of chickens; the cattle and sheep sickened and died. Everywhere was a shadow of death. The farmers spoke of much illness among their families.

35 In the town the doctors had become more and more puzzled by new kinds of sickness appearing among their patients. There had been several sudden and unexplained deaths, not only among adults but even among children, who would be stricken

40 suddenly while at play and die within a few hours.

There was a strange stillness. The birds, for example – where had they gone? Many people spoke of them,

45 puzzled and disturbed. The feeding stations in the backyards were deserted. The few birds seen anywhere trembled violently and could not fly. It was a spring without voices. On the mornings that had once throbbed

50 with the dawn chorus of robins, catbirds, doves, jays, wrens, and scores of other bird voices there was now no sound; only silence lay over the fields and woods and marsh.

On the farms the hens brooded, but no chicks hatched. The farmers complained that they were unable to raise any flocks

55 – the litters were small and the young survived only a few days. The apple trees were coming into bloom but no bees droned among the blossoms, so there was no pollination and there would be no fruit.

The roadsides, once so attractive, were now lined with browned

60 and withered vegetation as though swept by fire. These, too, were silent, deserted by all living things. Even the streams were now lifeless. Anglers no longer visited them, for all the fish had died.

In the gutters under the eaves and between the shingles of the

65 roofs, a white granular powder still showed a few patches; some weeks before it had fallen like snow upon the roofs and the lawns, the fields and streams. No enemy action had silenced

US farmworkers spraying locusts with pesticides in the 1950s

Glossary

prosperous successful or rich

blight disease that affects plants

maladies illness or diseases

pollination fertilization of a plant with pollen (usually by bees and insects)

wither become dried up and shrivelled

angler person who fishes with a rod and line

scores lots

stricken overcome or strongly affected by an illness or unpleasant feeling such as fear or grief

spectre ghost

- Examine closely how texts mirror the time and place in which they are written
- Explain how choosing certain language can enhance impact of writing
- Participate in group discussions and debates

the rebirth of new life in this stricken world. The people had done it themselves.

70 This town does not actually exist, but it might easily have a thousand counterparts in America or elsewhere in the world. I know of no community that has experienced all the misfortunes I describe. Yet every one of these disasters has actually happened somewhere, and many real communities have already suffered

75 a substantial number of them. A grim spectre has crept upon us almost unnoticed, and this imagined tragedy may easily become a stark reality we all shall know.

What has already silenced the voices of spring in countless towns in America? This book is an attempt to explain.

From *Silent Spring* by RACHEL CARSON

Comprehension

 A

1 What is the state of agricultural production and the landscape at the start of the extract?

2 What happened to the farmlands and environment once the 'blight' crept over the area? Support your answer with examples from the text.

3 What is hinted at as the possible source of the problem?

 B

1 What does the word 'once', short for 'once upon a time', suggest in the first line?

2 What literary technique is used in lines 9–12? Is it effective?

3 Analyze the paragraph structure, and comment on what is characteristic of the:

  a descriptions in the first two paragraphs

  b tone and focus from paragraph three

  c nature of a fable

  When do we get to the moral of the story?

 C

1 Why do you think Rachel Carson chose to introduce her work of scientific investigation as a fable or modern-day fairy tale?

Talk about ...

- What effect do you think Rachel Carson's *Silent Spring* had on public opinion when it was published in 1962?
- Do you think the issues described in her book are still relevant today?

Learning tip
A **fable** is a short story that tells a moral truth, often using animals as characters. Examples of famous fables are: *The Tortoise and the Hare*, *Peter and the Wolf* and *The Country Mouse and the City Mouse*.

• Examine and discuss a wide range of texts

The app that makes a difference

In honour of Inventors' Day, the American Society of Mechanical Engineers published a story on how young inventors aim to change the world.

One of the young inventors profiled was 15-year-old Emma Yang. Emma was born in Hong Kong and spent ten years there before moving to New York City. Her father was born in Beijing, China, and her mother grew up in Vietnam. When Emma was eight, her dad introduced her to the coding program Scratch.

Young inventors who change the world

Inventor: Emma Yang
Age: 15
Claim to fame: smartphone app Timeless

Emma Yang's grandmother suffers from Alzheimer's, an irreversible, progressive brain disorder that destroys memory and cognitive skills slowly over a long period of time. She wanted to help those that suffer from the disease to be able to
5 hold on to their memories.

At the age of 12, Yang created the smartphone app Timeless. She spent two years working on the app that uses AI-powered facial recognition to help Alzheimer's or dementia patients identify people in their life. Patients take a photo of a person
10 and the app helps them identify who that is, whether it is a loved one or a caregiver.

The app lets family and friends upload photos and pings the patient to view an updated feed where each photo is tagged with the person's name and categorized. The app also functions
15 as a daily planner and helps patients to remember events and stay connected to their social support system.

In 2015, Yang won first place at the Technovation Challenge in the US and second place globally. She was the youngest participant of the 2016 White House Opportunity Project,
20 representing Wolfram Research. She also won the 2018 Women Who Tech Startup Challenge, earning $50,000 for her company.

Yang is currently working with an international team of developers and Kairos to improve the app. Miami-based Kairos is the facial recognition AI software used in Timeless. Yang is
25 also attending high school in New York.

Glossary

app computer program designed to do a particular job, especially one you can use on a smartphone

AI (artificial intelligence) involves the use of computers to perform tasks normally requiring human intelligence

dementia brain disorder characterized by memory loss, confusion and personality changes

developer someone who thinks of or produces a new product, such as computer software

Comprehension

A

1 What personal motivation led Emma to invent the Timeless app?

2 Why is facial-recognition software useful to someone who suffers from Alzheimer's?

3 What other uses does the Timeless app have that help the user and their friends and family?

B

1 Identify the focus of each paragraph. For example, the opening paragraph explains Emma's grandmother's illness.

2 Look at your list of paragraph topics.

  a How does the use of personal experience help the first paragraph immediately engage the reader?

  b How do the topic choices for the other paragraphs help to retain the reader's interest and create a logical structure for the text?

C

1 Why do you think so many companies, healthcare providers and government agencies have supported the app?

2 How useful is Emma Yang's personal story to the development of the app?

3 Imagine you are an app developer who wants to create an app which is useful for society. Is it more important to have good technical knowledge, or to have an understanding of human (or user) experience? Explain your answer.

- Discuss ideas with others, questioning and evaluating opposing views
- Participate in group discussions and debates
- Look at how texts are structured and presented in order to influence the reader's point of view

Stretch zone

Think of other useful apps that have made a difference.

Do some research to find out how they were invented and put together a short presentation for your class or group explaining how the app was developed and by whom.

The match girls make a stand

This work of historical fiction is based on a real event that happened in 1888 at the Bryant & May match factory in Bow, London. The strike was led by a largely female workforce, many of whom were under 14 years of age since they were paid less than adult workers. The strike was motivated by this poor pay and unfair management practices, as well as the health risks of working with white phosphorus, which caused a life-threatening condition that often led to the facial deformity of 'phossy jaw', the first signs of which were toothache.

This extract is written from the point of view of a girl called Eliza, who has the courage to speak out and confront those in charge. The factory owner is Mr Wilkinson, and the foreman is Mr Fettler. As a result of the match girls' strike, questions are being asked in parliament about working conditions and pay in factories. Mr Wilkinson is furious that his reputation might be in danger. He has finally agreed to meet the match girls, and Eliza cleverly uses her powers of persuasion to make a lasting difference for the workers.

- Examine closely how texts mirror the time and place in which they are written
- Read literature about different historical periods
- Understand the meaning and effect of new and unfamiliar words

The real-life match girls

Eliza's triumph

I looked at Mr Wilkinson [...] and suddenly saw that he needed to be given a way out. A way that gave us what we wanted but that allowed him to keep his pride. He needed to be able to walk out of the meeting room looking and feeling like the
5   important gentleman he thought he was.

Just as I was thinking that, I noticed Mr Fettler hovering in the shadows by the door. And I saw a way of solving everything.

I turned to Mr Wilkinson. I made my face look as blank and as simple as I possibly could. All this time both sides had tried

- Examine closely how texts mirror the time and place in which they are written
- Read literature about different historical periods

10 to portray us as innocent, sheep-like girls being exploited by powerful people for their own ends. Well then, why not play that part, just for a bit?

"Can I say something, sir?" I said.

"Yes, of course," Mr Wilkinson replied. But he was looking a
15 bit suspicious, like he thought I was up to something.

I lowered my head as if I was in awe of him. And I said, as if I was truly puzzled and wanted him to explain things to me, "I'm thinking it's a shame how all this happened. It got so out of hand! But you seem like a fair-minded gentleman, Mr
20 Wilkinson. And a kind one, if I may be so bold. One who'd like to take care of the poor, ignorant girls he's got working for him. I don't understand how a fine, upstanding gentleman such as yourself would risk his workers catching phossy jaw just so he could save himself a few pennies. So I'm wondering
25 if maybe you didn't know about it? Can I ask, sir, does Mr Fettler tell you everything that goes on down on the factory floor? Or does he keep things like that to himself?"

It's an interesting thing, flattery. Say something nice to a girl and they won't believe you. The amount of times I'd told Nell
30 she was beautiful, only for her to go bright pink and bat away the compliment like I was teasing her! But say something flattering to a man, and he puffs himself up and purrs like a cat that's got the cream, even if what you're telling him is a blindingly obvious lie.

35 I could see the cogs turning in Mr Wilkinson's brain. He was flattered. And I was offering him a way out. A way to make concessions to us and yet retain his reputation. I was handing him someone to blame.

If Mr Wilkinson said he didn't know what had been going on,
40 why then […] he couldn't be accused of being a heartless, shameless exploiter of girls and young women, could he? No, […] if he made concessions now, he'd be seen as a generous protector. A good and kind employer, a sort of noble, selfless father figure to his workforce. Mr Wilkinson would look like
45 the respectable owner of a respectable factory and no doubt more people would choose to invest in it.

Glossary

foreman worker who supervises and directs other workers

exploited treated unfairly; offered very little in return for a lot of work

upstanding honest, respectable

flattery insincere or excessive praise

concession special privilege given to someone

And so he took the bait I was dangling before him.

"You're quite right," Mr Wilkinson said. He looked at Mr Fettler, assessing him, no doubt weighing up his usefulness, wondering
50 if he was worth hanging on to. Or not.

He suddenly announced to the whole room, "I see now that Mr Fettler hasn't kept me fully informed of problems on the factory floor. And I apologize most sincerely for that. I am very grateful that you have brought these matters to my attention.
55 Please be assured that the situation will be corrected. As for now, your demands shall, of course, be met."

That was it.

We'd won!

We. Had. Won.

60 There should have been fireworks. Trumpets sounding. [...]

Instead, there was an astonished pause. I knew the meeting would break up in a moment. I looked at Mr Fettler. He might get the sack, but if he did he'd be replaced by a man cut from the same cloth and we'd be back to square one. There was
65 something else we needed. I spoke fast.

"Can I propose something else too, sir?" I said. "How about the girls elect a representative? Maybe more than one – maybe a whole committee? Girls who can bypass the foreman and report straight to you. We can keep you informed, like. So
70 you'll get to hear about things straight from the horse's mouth, as it were. If anything crops up, we'll come to you, Mr Wilkinson, and you'll give us a fair hearing, won't you? We can nip any trouble in the bud, so things won't never go as far as another walk-out. How does that sound?"

75 Mr Wilkinson smiled at me kindly, the way a grandfather might smile on his granddaughter when he was giving her a treat. "That sounds perfectly reasonable," he said. "Agreed."

The look Mr Fettler gave me would have shrivelled a slug. It didn't much matter now whether he stayed or whether he got
80 the push. [...] All I could do was grin back at him.

From Lightning Strike *by* Tanya Landman

Do you think words or actions can make the biggest difference? Justify your answer.

Language tip

During this unit, you have encountered a variety of different sentence structures which are made up of different types of **clauses**.

Main clauses contain a subject and a verb and could stand alone as a sentence.

For example: 'The apple trees were coming into bloom but no bees droned ...' (page 154)

Subordinate clauses add additional information to the main clause using a subordinating conjunction. They cannot stand alone as a full sentence.

For example: 'I lowered my head as if I was in awe of him.' (page 159)

Relative clauses are a type of subordinate clause. They give additional information about a noun.

For example: 'Others came to fish the streams, which flowed clear and cold out of the hills.' (page 153)

Comprehension

1 What part does Eliza decide to play when talking to Mr Wilkinson? Why?
2 What question does Eliza ask Mr Wilkinson which gives him 'a way out'?
3 How does Mr Wilkinson want to appear to the outside world, especially those who might invest in his factory?
4 What else does Eliza realize the workers need? (lines 61–74)

1 Eliza uses several idiomatic phrases that refer to the animal kingdom. In your own words, explain what you think these mean:
   a 'innocent, sheep-like girls' (line 10)
   b 'purrs like a cat that's got the cream' (lines 32–33)
   c 'straight from the horse's mouth' (line 70)
   d 'would have shrivelled a slug' (line 78)
   Why might animal imagery be effective in this narrative?
2 How does Eliza use flattering language and persuasive techniques to make Mr Wilkinson agree to her demands? Find quotations to support your answer.
3 Think about the sentence structures used in the extract. Is Eliza's narrative style formal or informal? Explain your answer with examples from the text.

1 Reading the extract, what impression do you get of the social and political conditions of late-nineteenth-century England?
2 Do you think it is important to fictionalize historical events today? Why or why not?
3 Do you believe that persuasive words make a difference? Explain your answer.

Imagine you were there

Write your own short work of historical fiction to revisit an important event in history which caused great change to be enacted and imagine what it would have been like to be there as one of the participants.

- Research your chosen topic and find out as much as you can about those involved, and what their actions achieved.
- Try to show the perspective of someone living in that time and place.
- How useful is the benefit of hindsight (understanding something about an event after it has happened)?
- Share your writing with a partner and swap feedback.

- Identify evidence in a text about the environment, culture and social situation
- Explain how language and grammatical features enhance impact, create structure and contribute to the purpose of a text
- Carry out comprehensive research on a range of topics
- Understand and write from different points of view

Language tip
A **rhetorical question** is asked to make a point, rather than to get an answer. Here is an example from the text:

'Well then, why not play that part, just for a bit?'

Stretch zone
Find the following idioms in the text:
- 'get the sack'
- 'cut from the same cloth'
- 'be back to square one'
- 'nip any trouble in the bud'
- 'got the push'.

Write a short explanation of what you think each one means, and how it works to enhance meaning in the text.

How do you find your place in the world?

> The voice I hear this passing night was heard
> In ancient days by emperor and clown:
> Perhaps the self-same song that found a path
> Through the sad heart of Ruth, when, sick for home,
> She stood in tears amid the alien corn ...
>
> From 'Ode to a Nightingale' by JOHN KEATS

Talk about ...

- How do these lines from Keats capture what young people experience when they first come to live in another country?
- What kinds of pressures does moving country put on families?
- How long do you think it takes to feel at home in a new place?

When the English poet John Keats wrote of the figure of Ruth in the 'alien corn', he was describing a familiar scene to many who travel far away from the land that they grew up in.

Finding your way in a changing world is something we all have to deal with at some point in our lives. Growing up is often stressful for young people and their families. How much more difficult do you think it is for families who have made their home in another country? Have you or someone you know ever experienced this?

A difficult conversation

Young Ju is a teenager who emigrated from Korea to America with her parents when she was young. As a child, she thought they were on their way to heaven, but as she grows up, the difficulties become more apparent in the contrast between home life and fitting in and conforming at school. Here, she is trying to persuade her mother to allow her to go to her best friend's party on the beach.

Becoming too American

It is Amanda's first party. A beach birthday party. I can't go, Uhmma and Apa do not like it that my best friend is an American, a girl who might influence me in the wrong ways. Fast American ways. Supposedly, American girls do not study
5 and they do not think of anyone but themselves. Uhmma and Apa do not want me to end up like them.

"But Uhmma," I beg, following her down the hall to the kitchen. "It is her birthday."

"No, Young Ju, you can see her at school and give her your
10 gift then, but you don't need to go to the beach with her."

"Why?" I ask and slam my body into a chair. "Why, Uhmma? What is so wrong with going to the beach?"

"Always 'why' with you. Do not let your Apa hear those kinds of words. Already he has been complaining that you ask too
15 many questions. Young Ju, we will go to the beach another time," Uhmma says.

She pulls some scallions out of the refrigerator and rinses them off in the sink.

"That is not the same," I cry. "Amanda needs me at the party.
20 I am her best friend!"

As Uhmma carries the scallions to the cutting board near the sieve, she gives me a narrow-eyed glance. This is a sore subject. I change my tactics.

"Uhmma, Amanda has been so nice to me. When I missed
25 school from that cold, she gave me all her notes from class."

Glossary

Uhmma Korean word for 'Mama'

Apa Korean word for 'Papa'

sieve mesh filter used to separate smaller from larger parts

tactics methods used to achieve something or gain an advantage

- Find evidence in a text about the environment, culture and social situation
- Discuss the meaning of new and unfamiliar words

"That is nice," Uhmma says and chops the scallions in half. "And when it was my birthday she got me this necklace," I say and pull out from under my shirt collar my half of the 'Friends Forever' heart necklace.

30 Uhmma presses her lips together but does not look in my direction. She lines up the halves of the scallions and starts to chop. Fine slivers of green and white circles cover the cutting board.

35 I slump in my seat and say, "And when I did not have any lunch money, she let me borrow some from her."

"What!" Uhmma stops chopping in mid-motion, knife raised in the air.

"Nothing," I quickly say.

40 "What did you say, Young Ju?" Uhmma waves the knife in the air. I scratch my cheek, look up at the ceiling, sigh.

"When I did not have any lunch money and we ran out of bread last week, Amanda let me borrow some money."

"Young Ju, how could you do this?" Uhmma cries, putting down the knife. "You took money from Ah-man-dah!" Uhmma asks.

45 "Yes," I say. "She is my friend and she said I could borrow it."

"Now you are obligated to her." Uhmma leans her hip against the counter.

"I am not obligated to her, Uhmma. I am going to pay her back."

50 "Young Ju, have I not taught you never to take from others? Do not make yourself obligated to another person."

"Uhmma, she is my friend." I stand up and wave my arms in the air. "This is America. In America it is fine to borrow money from friends."

55 "Stop that," Uhmma says. "We are Korean. Do not forget."

I sit back down. "Korean. Then why did we move to America?"

"You can go to the party," Uhmma says.

Glossary

sliver thin slip or slice of something
obligated owe gratitude to someone who has helped you
pier structure built out into the sea for people to walk on

● Find evidence in a text about the environment, culture and social situation

I'm so stunned I'm not sure I heard correctly. Did she say I could go?

60 "What?" I ask.

"You must fulfil your obligation for inconveniencing her. Also, you will pay her back the money you borrowed." Uhmma shakes her head. "Have I not taught you anything? After this, do not take anything from her. Understand?"

65 "Yes, Uhmma."

I jump out of my chair to get ready for the party before she has a chance to change her mind.

As Uhmma drives towards the pier, I can see a group of kids from school in the far distance. I turn to Uhmma.

70 "Stop, Uhmma. You can drop me off here."

The station wagon's brakes groan and then squeal in a high-pitched scream as Uhmma comes to a stop near the curb. Uhmma squints at the kids.

"Are those not your friends over there?"

75 I turn my head away from her and look out my window at the long stretch of sand.

I lie softly, "That is another group. You can drop me off here and I will look around for Amanda. She said they would be near the pier."

80 "Are you sure you will be able to find them?" Uhmma worries.

I open the car door and toss back, "Do not worry, Uhmma, I know where to find them. Remember that Amanda is going to drop me off at home and you do not have to come back and get me."

85 "Yes, I will remember," Uhmma says.

I step out of the car and wave goodbye. Uhmma leans across the passenger seat giving me a finger shake.

"Young Ju, do not forget to give Ah-man-dah the money you borrowed. Be a polite girl and help her
90 parents with the party."

> **Learning tip**
> **Animating the dialogue**
> There are many ways to animate dialogue in fictional writing and other texts. They include using:
>
> - dialogue tags to help the reader identify who is speaking
>
> For example: "Yes," <u>I say</u>.
>
> - adverbs and adjectives that describe movement to add tone and mood
>
> For example: "Nothing," I <u>quickly</u> say, feeling <u>hesitant</u>.
>
> When it is obvious who is speaking, you don't have to use a dialogue tag at all.

165

I hold the door, ready to slam it shut.

"Yes, Uhmma," I say, waving again. "Bye."

Uhmma waves back. "Have a nice time, Young Ju."

95 I shut the door and walk away. The station wagon sputters as Uhmma presses on the gas pedal. I know without turning around that there are dark clouds of smoke streaming from the muffler.

From *A Step From Heaven* by An Na

- Find evidence in a text about the environment, culture and social situation
- Examine how a writer's use of language and grammatical features creates effect and meaning
- Write non-fiction texts, including autobiographies and letters

Comprehension

1 What do you think is meant here by 'fast American ways', and how does this define the difficult conversation between mother and daughter in this extract? (line 4)

2 Why does Young Ju's mother finally give her permission to go to Amanda's beach party?

3 Explain Young Ju's deception at the end of the text.

1 Why do you think the writer spells 'Amanda' as 'Ah-man-dah' when it is spoken by Young Ju's mother?

2 Analyze the conversation in this extract and identify five:

a dialogue tags used in the conversation between Young Ju and her mother

b short sentences or phrases that describe the action, tone or movement that animate the dialogue

1 How do cultural differences make the divisions between parents and their teenage children especially hard to deal with?

I'd like some advice ...

Write a short letter to an advice page of an online magazine. Talk about a difficulty, dilemma or misunderstanding that has occurred in a family relationship.

- You can use the situation and characters from the above extract, or create your own.
- Use emotive and expressive language to explain your frustrations, any distress caused, and how much you want to improve the relationship and situation.

 Stretch zone

Swap letters with someone else in your class or group, and write a letter of reply as it would appear in the magazine. Keep it short and positive.

A daughter tries to help her mother

Alice Pung, the writer of the following text, was born in Melbourne in Australia. Her Chinese-Cambodian parents had made the perilous journey to leave Cambodia when the country was ruled by Pol Pot in the 1970s.

Alice (called Agheare by her family) identifies with both worlds: the world of her family's history and culture, and the Australian world of school and friends into which she was born. But it is much harder for her mother.

- Find evidence in a text about the environment, culture and social situation
- Discuss the meaning of new and unfamiliar words

Learning English in Australia in the 1970s/1980s

Learning the English

The quieter I became at school the louder my mother became at home. She was loud because she could not read or speak the secret talk we knew. She could not read because she had been housebound for two decades. And now, over the dinner
5   table, she would watch as my father and his children littered their language with English terms, until every second word was in the foreign tongue. We hardly noticed the food which she had prepared for us, so engrossed were we in our babble. She sat there staring at us, trying to make sense of these aliens
10   at her table.

"Migrants don't assimilate," I was told by classmates in politics class. "They all come here and stick together, and don't bother to learn the language." But I remembered when my mother bundled all four of us into the car after school. "Agheare," she
15   told me. "Look at the map. Find this place for me. Your father gave me the address. I am going to learn the English. I am going

Glossary

litter scatter around a place

engrossed completely focused on a task or activity

assimilate become integrated into a society

incredulously unwilling to believe something

blazer light jacket often worn as part of school uniform

discreet careful in what you say, not giving anything away

• Find evidence in a text about the environment, culture and social situation

to learn it now, no matter what." We did not even change out of our uniforms, there was no time. My mother decided that if she knew the English, all her problems would be solved, she would
20 be able to do anything in this new country. Most of all, she would be able to enter the world of her children's minds.

We pulled up in front of a community centre and were met by a kind woman with a lilting British accent, hair like a soft grey felt hat on her head, grey flannel scarf and kind grey
25 eyes. She looked like an old wise possum and she invited us all into the centre for coffee before our discussion. My mother's heart melted. We all sat round a table strewn with newspapers and books.

"So it says here that your mother is forty," said the woman
30 incredulously.

Until then, I didn't even know my mother's age. I asked her, and she nodded.

"Unbelievable! She looks twenty!" I repeated this to my mother. She signed up for the class straightaway.

An Australian possum

35 My mother asked us to speak to her in English. I did so, slowly and carefully. I asked her questions: "How are you? How was your day?" But because these were questions Chinese children never asked their parents, even if she had enough words to answer me, she would not have known how. "Stop asking me
40 crazy, pointless questions," she said, "and let me learn something useful!"

"Alright, Ma. What do you want to learn? What do you want to talk about?"

"You tell me! You're the teacher now!" She looked at me as
45 if I had all the answers and was keeping them from her from some perverse whim, as if I had them hidden in the inside pocket of my blazer.

The migrants in her class were all at different levels, and my mother could not understand the worksheets. She dumped all
50 her notebooks and worksheets on the floor of her room.

"Well, this stuff might be too hard," I said, discreetly shoving the piles of paper under her bed. "Why don't you start from the very beginning?" I picked up my five-year-old sister's school reader. "Pat is … a … cat," my mother read. "He is a

The roots of ginseng

55 black and white cat." Her fingers, gnarled as just-dug-up
ginseng, pointed at each word. She could read the whole book
through not once, not twice, but three times. She sighed a big
sigh. "Ah, it's no use. No use! It is all useless, I don't understand
a thing."

60 "But Ma, you just read the whole book through three times."

"No, I didn't!"

"Yes, you did!"

She turned to the middle pages and pointed. "I don't know
what it says. I just memorized the whole thing when you first
65 read it out to me. Don't teach me any more. Go off and study."

From *Unpolished Gem* by ALICE PUNG

- Examine how a writer's use of language and grammatical features creates effect and meaning
- Explain how an author develops character, setting and plot

Comprehension

A

1 Why did the writer's mother feel that her family had become 'aliens at her table'?

2 Why are the questions the writer asks her mother inappropriate?

3 How would learning English help the writer's mother?

4 What qualities in the mother's character make it difficult for her to learn English?

B

1 What does the word 'assimilate' in line 11 mean? How does this extract contradict the point being made about migrants refusing to assimilate?

2 Explain the idiom used in lines 26–27: 'My mother's heart melted.'

3 What is a 'perverse whim' in line 46? How does it help to explain the confused relationship between mother and daughter?

4 Explain the following two similes:
   a 'like an old wise possum' (line 25)
   b 'gnarled as just-dug-up ginseng' (lines 55–56)

C

1 What does this extract explain about the success and failure of the family's assimilation into Australian society?

Talk about ...

- What kind of problems are the families in 'Learning the English' and 'Becoming too American' experiencing?
- What do you think the family members could do to improve the situations in the two texts?
- What special difficulties do the children of migrants face in their teenage years? What divided loyalties might they experience?

Establishing a foothold in a new country

The writer of the following poem describes the experience of her family who left Damascus in Syria for a new life in Utah, in the Midwest of the United States. Pay attention to the analogy with a fantastical giant bird from Arabian mythology.

- Consider how poets play with different themes and conventions
- Discuss the meaning of new and unfamiliar words
- Investigate the origin of words

The Roc

Here's my mom and dad leaving
    all familiar signposts: Damascus, the streets they knew,
    measurement of time in mosque sounds,
    the regular scrape of heavy wooden shutters,
5 the daily boiling and cooling of fresh milk.
    Anyone back home who had no phone fell off
    the disc of their new world: tomato-cart man,
    schoolchildren in skittish flocks. Crazy Fat'ma
    the Goatwoman, all the newly married cousins,
10 the porter at the door they left behind.

Here they are crossing the world,
hoisting up all they know like a sail,
landing in Utah. The time is March 15, 1971.

They know nothing about America:
15   how to grocery shop,
    how to open a bank account,
    how the milk comes, thin glass bottles
    on tin chinking them awake,
what 'you bet' or 'sure thing' meant
20   in real spoken English, outside
    the London-grammar books so creased,
    so carefully underlined. It was,
    my mother said, as if a monstrous bird
had seized them up and dropped
25   them in a fantastic terrain.

Here's my mother studying
the instructions on the coin-
box of a laundry machine,
enrolling us in kindergarten,

30 tape-recording her college lectures so
    that she could play, replay, decode
    the stream of alien phonemes into words.

Word origins

phoneme (n), from the ancient Greek *phonema*, meaning 'sound' or 'speech'
Related words:
- telephone
- phonics

Glossary

Roc bird from Arabian mythology. Marco Polo described Rocs living in Madagascar, and Sinbad the Sailor in *The Arabian Nights* described seeing one which 'blotted out the sun' on his second voyage after he had found the 'great white dome' of a gigantic egg. The Roc was said to feed its young on elephants.

skittish frisky, lively, excitable

phoneme linguistic term for a unit of sound that cannot be broken down further

native someone or something from a particular place

subsidize pay a subsidy to a person or organization

merchandise goods for sale

vertigo feeling of dizziness or loss of balance

transmission a broadcast

That's her refolding foil, stretching the little
    budget over the month, making the
35   ten-cent toys our treasures of Sinbad.

Here's my father staking
    his life's savings on one semester.
He works hard and at the end of the term,
    on the day before the last dollar
40   of the life savings is gone,
    he walks into the Chair's office
    and the Chair gives him a job teaching.
Other friendly natives explain
    subsidized student housing,
45   coupons, and the good places to find
    bargain basement merchandise.

The pilgrims were so happy
at being shown how to survive here
    after the first long winter,
50   they had a feast. That's mom,
    laughing at the strange loaf of bread.
    There's dad holding up the new world coffee
in its funny striped boxes. That's us,
    small, weightless, wobbly
55   with the vertigo of the newly landed
    voyager.

Here they are, mom and dad,
    telephoning back home, where the folks
    gather around the transmission
60   as if it was from the moon.
    The phone call to Syria was
    for epic events only. The line pulsates
as if with the beating of enormous wings.
They shout and shout into the receiver
65   as if the other end were ages
    and ages away. Spiny talon
    digs into rock.

MOHJA KAHF

The Roc, which fed its young on elephants

171

Comprehension

1 What familiar sights and sounds did the writer's parents leave behind in Damascus?

2 What unfamiliar practices and experiences do they encounter in their new life?

3 How do the writer's mother and father ensure that the family survive financially?

1 How does the metaphor of the Roc relate to the family's experience of arriving in a strange land?

2 Identify the passages in the poem that extend the metaphor of the Roc and explain the effect.

3 Analyze the point of view of the writer. What is her perspective on the events that have taken place? At what point in her life is she writing?

1 Why do you think the writer adopts the point of view of an omniscient narrator?

2 How does this omniscient perspective work effectively with the analogy of the Roc?

- Consider how poets play with themes and conventions
- Understand how a point of view is conveyed in a text
- Explain how language and grammatical features enhance impact, create structure and contribute to the purpose of a text

Language tip

An **analogy** is a literary device in which two unrelated things are compared to create an image in the reader's mind, to suggest deeper meaning, and to help explain one or both of the things.

An analogy intends to make a point about something, differing from metaphor or simile, which just show a comparison.

Stretch zone

What other analogies can you think of for moving from one country to another?

Language tip
Omniscient narrator

Writing from an **omniscient** (or all-seeing and all-knowing) perspective allows the writer to show the thoughts, feelings and actions of all characters, and what is happening at all points of a narrative.

This contrasts with a **limited narrator**, where the narrator relates only their own thoughts, feelings and knowledge.

A Syrian family shopping in a US supermarket

Moving to a new place

Now write your own poem or short prose text about the experience of moving to another place. You could describe moving countries, moving from a rural to an urban location, or moving from the centre of the city to an outer suburb. It can be fictional or based on a real experience.

- Set the scene and describe where you are living now and how it compares to where you came from. What is most striking about your new place?
- Use an analogy as in the poem 'The Roc'. It could be a mythological character or a superhero, or some representative persona that you adopt to reflect upon your new situation.
- Decide on the voice and perspective you will take. Will you write from the first-, second- or third-person point of view, and will your narrator be limited or omniscient?
- Make use of literary devices such as alliteration, metaphor, simile, personification, repetition, onomatopoeia, or any others you like.

Share your writing with a partner and offer each other feedback.

- Write a range of fiction genres and poetry
- Use literary and rhetorical devices to enhance the impact of writing

Stretch zone

Storyboard or create a photo narrative to describe your move. Make sure to include captions that animate your image library with useful anecdotes and supporting reflections presented in a consistent voice.

Returning home to Bosnia

The writer of the following text left her home town of Mostar in Bosnia in 1992 at the start of the Bosnian War. She was 16 and still at school. The text describes her return home to Bosnia after four years, during which time she had adapted to life in the UK.

View of the Stari Most Bridge across the Neretva River in Mostar. The old bridge stood for 427 years until it was destroyed on 9 November 1993 during the Bosnian War. It has since been reconstructed.

Coming home

You enter Croatia at around 4 a.m. and it feels like the most beautiful moment in your life. The air is a deep bruise-blue, a round moon hangs in the sky and the sea reflects its white light in small ripples. That part of the coast is your favourite, where
5   small barren islands look like mercury dropped in water. The coach pulls into Split station at 10 a.m. and, as the door opens, smells of the sea, fish, coffee and traffic mingle and travel inside. You are taking everything in slowly, separating each scent strand in your nostrils, savouring all of them, even those that
10 would usually make you feel sick.

You take your hefty backpack and pull its bulk on the ground to the nearest table read order an espresso. The air is warm, the sun is shining and the sky is an endless spread of blue,

- Discuss the meaning of new and unfamiliar words
- Explain how an author develops character, setting and plot

15 blending with the sea. You sip your coffee, and then another and another. You are starting to feel giddy with caffeine and the numb exhaustion of the journey falls away into the background. You wash your face in the sink of the cramped white tiled bathroom. You leave your bag in a plastic white kiosk where an elderly lady looks after it for a bit of money, and you secretly

20 hope someone will steal it, but you know no one would steal such a heavy, cheap-looking backpack. You walk down the buzzing street, among the jewellery and souvenir stands, down into the post office where you buy a telephone card.

"Hello Mama!" you say into the small holes of the plastic
25 receiver.

"Darling! You are here! How are you? How was your journey?" Your mother is ecstatic and you are happy to hear that she is so happy.

You dial another number. It's one of your best friends, who
30 doesn't know you're coming. You walk back to the station to board your bus for home, full of memories triggered by almost everything around you, impatience boiling in your chest to get home. The voices of your mother and your friend are still climbing up and down the walls of your brain and you go over the
35 conversations, wondering how you sounded, trying to imagine your own voice in their ears, and wondering if they were thinking about you for as long as you were thinking about them.

People have told you that the city is unrecognizable:
100 per cent damage, which apparently means that
40 every building in the city was damaged. The old bridge has gone, houses are gone, streets are rubble. But you don't want to think about that, not yet. As the bus struggles down the winding road to the valley in which your home town sits, everything looks the same. You
45 also heard that from people. "When you're approaching, it looks just the same. You can't see any damage." Two old women are asking you how long it's been since you've been home. You tell them four years and they nod their heads with sympathy. "It was hard
50 here my dear, you did well not to be around," one of them says. You agree.

Glossary

mercury heavy, silvery metal used in thermometers and barometers

hefty heavy, large and strong

giddy feeling that everything is spinning and you might fall

triggered started something happening

rubble pieces of brick or stone

Lilliputian adjective from Lilliput, the island in the 1726 English novel *Gulliver's Travels* by Jonathan Swift, where people are only about six inches (15cm) tall

A bomb-damaged building in Mostar

55

The bus stops at the second stop in the city, your stop, and you see your mother waiting for you, craning her neck to see where you are. You get out, take your bag and throw yourself in her arms. You hug each other as if your life depends on it, trying to squeeze as much comfort as you can out of each other, trying to blend into each other. You walk down the street towards your home, and you are struck by something unexpected – everything looks smaller. The streets look narrower, the houses Lilliputian,

60

and you realize you have grown. It is difficult to get a grip on the time that has passed. Everything has been frozen in your memory since you left and now everything is different.

From *Bluebird: A Memoir* by VESNA MARIC

- Present personal opinions clearly and succinctly with confidence
- Understand and write from a particular viewpoint

The ancient Greek philosopher Heraclitus (c.540–480 BCE) is believed to have said that we can never step twice into the same river. People also often say, "You can't go home again". Both of these ideas suggest that things will always be different when you go back somewhere after being away. Do you agree? Do you think it's a good thing that people and places change, or would you rather everything stayed the same?

Comprehension

1 How does the writer capture her first impressions of Croatia on arrival in Split?

2 What are the writer's thoughts and feelings as she gets closer to her final destination?

3 What is so unexpected and different about the writer's first sight of Mostar?

4 How have the years since the outbreak of the war changed the writer's perspective?

1 a Why do you think the writer uses the second-person pronoun 'you' instead of 'I' to tell her story?

   b What is the effect of this?

2 Find examples in the first paragraph of how the writer uses some of the five senses to evoke feelings and images for the reader.

1 How does the writer's use of perspective and tense suggest that her experience is shared by many other people?

2 How difficult do you think it is for the writer to be returning to her home town after so much has changed?

Stretch zone

Choose one or two paragraphs from the extract and rewrite them from either a first-person or third-person perspective. How does this change the effect the writing has on the reader?

Try also changing the tense from present to past, and notice the difference in effect.

Write about your return

Look at the painting below. What do you think of the title? How effective is the painting?

Now write a reflection on the experience of returning to a place you once knew well. Perhaps it was your first home, or a place you remember from early childhood.

- Look at your chosen place with fresh eyes and describe how it appears to you now.
- Pay particular attention to your thoughts and feelings upon your return. How has the place changed, and how have you changed?
- Include photographs, artworks, or other illustrations, such as images from your childhood and early family life, presented alongside contemporary views. You could take inspiration from Sara Hayward's painting.

Share your writing and images with a partner or group and ask for feedback.

Coming Home by Sara Hayward, showing the artist's home town in Cornwall, England

- Write non-fiction texts, including autobiographies and letters

Learning tip
Does a picture paint a thousand words? When you write about your return to a familiar place, do you also think of it in pictorial terms (do you see it as a picture or series of pictures in your head)? Make sure to use strong visual language to describe your thoughts and impressions in your writing.

Why is fashion important to us?

> 'Vain trifles as they seem, clothes change our view of the world and the world's view of us.'
>
> From *Orlando* by VIRGINIA WOOLF

Talk about …

- Do you think what you wear is important?
- What do someone's clothes say about them?
- What styles of clothing are in fashion at the moment where you live?
- When you buy new clothes, do you know who has made them?

How do the clothes you wear represent your identity and your outlook on life? Across the world, and in any one country or community, our fashion choices help to define us as individuals and as part of a social group.

Some fashion, such as clothes produced by famous designers, is too expensive for many people to afford. Other fashion is produced cheaply on a large scale, making it more affordable. We are more aware today of how we can help the environment by opting for sustainable or recycled fashion, and how we can help workers' rights by supporting clothing companies that provide acceptable working conditions in their factories. Think about these issues and your feelings about them as you work through the texts in this unit.

Glossary

fashion style of clothing that is popular at a particular time

How do clothes define our view of the world?

When you decide what to wear, do you think about how you are presenting yourself to the world? Even something as simple as how you wear and treat your school uniform (if you have one), or your everyday clothes, can make a difference to how you feel about yourself and how others perceive you.

Lucy Lam is a scholarship student at the prestigious Ladies' College, Laurinda, in Melbourne, Australia. It is a very different experience to her former high school in a less well-off neighbourhood. In this extract from the opening of the novel, she describes her first day at her new school.

Written like a diary, this is an example of an epistolary novel as each chapter takes the form of a letter with an addressee called 'Linh', who appears as an absent friend or *alter ego*.

- Compare and contrast a wide range of texts on the same theme
- Understand the meaning and effect of new and unfamiliar words

Learning tip

An **epistolary novel** is a work of fiction that is written in the form of letters or other documents. Epistolary novels can read like diaries, providing the opportunity for more personal thoughts and reflections.

An **alter ego** is a Latin term that means 'other self' and is used to describe a different version of oneself, which might be imagined as an intimate and trusted friend.

First day at Laurinda

Dear Linh, on my first day, when I entered our homeroom, I had no idea where to sit, so I headed for the first empty seat I saw, next to a girl with very long hair braided into a plait and a Madeira-cake face flecked with freckles.

5 "You're the new girl, aren't you?" she asked.

"Yes – how did you know?"

"All your clothes are new."

I looked down, embarrassed. Not a thread of my new uniform had been in the wash. My shirt had crease lines from being
10 folded in the packet. Around the room, the other girls' clothes had a lived-in, everyday look. Later, I would see how they chucked their jackets on the back seats of buses, tied their jumpers around their waists, not caring if the sleeves stretched, and hiked up the hems of their summer skirts. No one wore the
15 blue hair ribbons – I was the only one dumb enough to have taken that part of the uniform code seriously.

The girl next to me was named Katie. "Don't worry," she told me, "you look great."

I didn't detect any sarcasm. She was being genuinely kind, and
20 at that moment I learned two things about Katie. By telling

Glossary

Madeira cake classic British sponge cake, made with butter and lemon

sarcasm use of irony or cutting remarks to express disapproval or contempt

- Compare and contrast a wide range of texts on the same theme

me that she noticed my clothes were new, she was honest, but she could also tell the occasional white lie if the circumstances called for it.

After homeroom, we marched to the Performing Arts Centre
25 for assembly. Years Seven and Eight sat level with the stage, while Years Nine and Ten sat in the raised seating areas. Looking down, I could see a moving blanket of blue and maroon. I had never seen something so ordered before in real life, something so ... well, uniform.

30 Even though we had a uniform at the previous school, we got away with wearing whatever socks we wanted as long as they were white, and whatever shirt we wanted as long as it was blue. Remember how some girls came in with Esprit shirts, while others pulled their socks so high that they looked like
35 tights, Linh? Here, every girl in the auditorium had her hair tied back if it was below shoulder length. Here, every girl wore a blazer. Here, every girl sat still, no matter how long she had to wait. If she couldn't sit still, she was probably told to sit on her hands, as I saw many of the Year Sevens doing. I had been
40 to assemblies before, but this was the model of an assembly. Suddenly, I understood what it was to *assemble*, just as a few moments before I had truly understood *uniform*.

I heard the sound of bagpipes, and everyone began to stand. Then I saw a girl playing *actual* bagpipes march
45 through the stained-glass double doors of the auditorium.

Following her were two girls carrying long white flags emblazoned with the Laurinda motto – one in Latin (*Concordia Prorsum*) and the other in English (*Forward in Harmony*). They had more badges and pins on their
50 lapels than a World War Two veteran. Following them were four girls carrying red, blue, yellow and green flags. These, I presumed, were the house captains.

Finally, the staff of the college marched by, all decked out in black academic gowns. Some had sashes of
55 green or orange, while others had tassels and other scholarly insignia.

From Lucy and Linh by ALICE PUNG

Glossary

house captain student leadership role in a school

sash strip of cloth worn around the shoulders and waist

tassel bundle of threads tied together at the top

insignia badges or symbols showing membership or rank

- Explain how an author develops character, setting and plot
- Look at how texts are structured and presented in order to influence the reader's point of view
- Understand different points of view in a text

Comprehension

A

1 What is awkward or uncomfortable about being 'new' and wearing new clothes?

2 What kinds of 'model' behaviour does Lucy find so remarkable about Laurinda students?

3 Find all the references to military style and ceremony in the description of Lucy's first day.

B

1 **a** What do you think is meant by the reference to Katie's 'Madeira-cake face'?

   b How are colours and colour terms used to expand on themes in the extract?

2 Explain the following idiomatic phrases:

   a an 'occasional white lie'

   b to 'be decked out in' a particular fashion

C

1 Why is Lucy's analysis of the school uniform code useful in setting the scene?

2 How will her understanding of this code help her to fit in at her new school?

> **Stretch zone**
>
> Make a list of other epistolary texts that you have read and consider the role of the addressee (or addressees) in each case.

Analyzing a uniform code

Do you sometimes need to wear a uniform? It may not be a school uniform – perhaps you wear special clothes when you play in a sports team, or volunteer for a charity.

Write a short analysis of a uniform code at a school, club or community group that you belong to, or that you know of. Think about the following points:

- What is the dress code and what practical purpose does it serve?
- How are different members of the group identified?
- Does everyone conform? Or do people adapt or bend the rules? How?

Include detailed observations and personal reflections as part of your account. Share your analysis with your partner or group.

Between two cultures

This poem is by Moniza Alvi, who was born in Lahore, Pakistan, and now lives in England. The poem explores the confused feelings of a teenage girl who, like the author, is half-English, and lives between two cultures.

Presents from My Aunts in Pakistan

They sent me a salwar kameez
peacock-blue,
and another
glistening like an orange split open,
5   embossed slippers, gold and black
points curling.
Candy-striped glass bangles
snapped, drew blood.
Like at school, fashions changed
10   in Pakistan –
the salwar bottoms were broad
and stiff, then narrow.
My aunts chose an apple-green sari,
silver-bordered
15   for my teens.

I tried each satin-silken top –
was alien in the sitting-room.
I could never be as lovely
as those clothes –
20   I longed
for denim and corduroy.
My costume clung to me
and I was aflame,
I couldn't rise up out of its fire,
25   half-English,
unlike Aunt Jamila.

I wanted my parents' camel-skin lamp –
switching it on in my bedroom,
to consider the cruelty
30   and the transformation
from camel to shade,
marvel at the colours
like stained glass.

Glossary

salwar kameez traditional Pakistani outfit which generally consists of three pieces: a pair of long pants (**salwar** or **shalwar**), a top or shirt (**kameez**), and a scarf (**dupatta**)

embossed flat surface with a raised design

- Compare and contrast a wide range of texts on the same theme
- Consider how poets play with themes and conventions
- Discuss the meaning of new and unfamiliar words

My mother cherished her jewellery –
35 Indian gold, dangling, filigree,
But it was stolen from our car.
The presents were radiant in my wardrobe.
My aunts requested cardigans
from Marks and Spencers.

40 My salwar kameez
didn't impress the schoolfriend
who sat on my bed, asked to see
my weekend clothes.
But often I admired the mirror-work,
45 tried to glimpse myself
in the miniature
glass circles, recall the story
how the three of us
sailed to England.
50 Prickly heat had me screaming on the way.
I ended up in a cot
In my English grandmother's dining-room,
found myself alone,
playing with a tin-boat.

55 I pictured my birthplace
from fifties' photographs.
When I was older
there was conflict, a fractured land
throbbing through newsprint.
60 Sometimes I saw Lahore –
my aunts in shaded rooms,
screened from male visitors,
sorting presents,
wrapping them in tissue.

65 Or there were beggars, sweeper-girls
and I was there –
of no fixed nationality,
staring through fretwork
at the Shalimar Gardens.

MONIZA ALVI

Glossary

radiant radiating light or heat
fracture break something, especially a bone
fretwork carved ornamental work in wood

- Find evidence in a text about the environment, culture and social situation
- Participate fully in discussions

Comprehension

1 How does the poet communicate her experience of living between two cultures through her discussion of clothes?

2 Find references to difficult or painful associations in the text and explain them in context.

1 How does the poet's descriptions of the clothes, accessories and furnishings from Pakistan capture their 'alien' and 'exotic' quality? Find key examples in the text.

2 Find examples of compound words or phrases in the text and explain how they add value to the description.

3 Write your own compound phrase using a hyphen to describe a favourite item of clothing.

1 How does this poem highlight the poet's growing self-awareness and pride in her mixed cultural heritage?

Language tip

Hyphens are often used to create **compound phrases**. Here are two examples that modify a noun:

- 'distressed-denim jeans'
- 'rose-coloured silk'

These phrases add additional information and increase the descriptive power of the text.

Talk about ...

Think of a gift of clothing that you have received. How did you feel about the gift and were you comfortable wearing it?

Shalimar Gardens, Lahore, Pakistan

Diary of a fashion designer

- Examine and discuss a wide range of texts
- Investigate the origin of words

The British fashion designer Vivienne Westwood is well-known for making radical fashion statements and taking a 'do-it-yourself' approach to fashion. As a climate activist and campaigner for social justice, she is critical of the fashion industry and consumer lifestyles and her designs are never conventional. In this extract from her published diary, she explains her design process.

Vivienne Westwood

World Wide Woman

Tuesday 15 March 2011

I was so carried away by my last Gold Label show that I have decided to describe in some detail how a collection is formed.

5   Sometimes I know the idea for a collection but this time I started really late with no idea except for a fragment of a precious ribbon I had seen pictured in an old sales catalogue I discovered among my books. I wanted to get a copy woven, a ribbon I could cut up into same-size pieces and sew on to
10 T-shirts instead of graphics. I thought I'd love to wear a bit of old fabric instead of a slogan for a change. The original was medieval and the design had such a feeling of that time, formalized eagles in silk and gold threads. [...]

  Our prototypes are done in our Battersea studio but our
15 production is in Italy, so I asked our studio there to find a ribbon factory. Then I had to choose fabrics which they had pre-selected from the fabric fair. The less fabric the better, I think; too many and the possible permutations become endless as the ideas gather, and I like to 'cook' with basic ingredients. I kept to basic
20 fabrics; with some, I let in the natural colour of the fibre as it comes from the loom. For other plain fabrics I stuck to black, grey, indigo, brown, flesh, cream, white. Set against the fabrics we took gold, a lamé-looking like metal – gold sequins.

25 I love our toiles, our prototypes which we make in the natural calico before we decide the final fabric; it's as if the garment captures the first idea of itself. I took a very conservative man's tailoring fabric (I love conservative fabrics – they have so many ideas to play with), a

Word origins

couture (n), borrowed from French and comes from the Latin word *consuere*, meaning 'to sew up'; describes the business of designing, making and selling custom-fitted clothes for high-paying individual clients

Glossary

toile type of fine linen or cotton fabric used to test out a design or pattern before it is made with more expensive materials

185

- Present personal opinions clearly and succinctly with confidence
- Participate fully in discussions

30   fresco in grey chalk stripe, and made a suit comprising a jacket from two years back and a favourite skirt. […]

Plain fabrics show off the cut of the clothes. I like to mix garments from different times and places: historical, ethnic, twentieth-century couture – I copied a coat from Balenciaga and a dress

35   from Chanel. I sometimes copy from myself, re-doing clothes from way back in my archive. I like new things as well as things repeated and developed from last season. Most of all, I like 'do it yourself', as if the wearer has spontaneously put her own creation together in an afternoon.

40   I introduced colour by printing. Until recently printing was done only on screens or rollers but now we also have digital printing. The cost of full colour is less because it is all done in one go. There is no setting up cost so you might as well have every print different. That's what I did and found every print in my small

45   booklet of fabrics from the Museum of Fine Arts, Boston.

From *Get a Life: The Diaries of Vivienne Westwood 2010–2016* by
VIVIENNE WESTWOOD

Glossary

slogan short, snappy phrase used to promote a political cause

prototype first model of something, from which others are copied or developed

permutation way in which a set or number of things can be arranged

calico plain, white, cotton cloth

comprising including or consisting of

Comprehension

A

1 What kind of inspiration does Vivienne Westwood find in 'conservative' or traditional textile fabrics?

2 What quality does Westwood imagine for the ideal wearer of her fashion?

3 What things does Westwood mix and copy to create different outfits?

B

1 How does Westwood use the metaphor of 'cooking' to explain the process of designing a collection? (line 19)

2 What do you think is meant by the comment 'it's as if the garment captures the first idea of itself'? (lines 26–27)

C

1 Why do you think Westwood is so fond of the 'do-it-yourself' approach to fashion? (lines 37–38)

2 What do you think about this approach?

 Stretch zone

Look up this collection or any other garment or collection by Vivienne Westwood online and write your own short review of the look she has achieved. Identify, if you can, the different styles and materials she reuses.

Talk about …

Do you have a favourite fashion designer? Why do you like their designs?

Read an industry magazine

This short designer profile tells the story behind 19-year-old Joey Luciano's line of upcycled fashion that sold out almost immediately when it was released online. The profile was published in a print and online magazine aimed at readers working in the textile and clothing industries.

- Examine and discuss a wide range of texts
- Find evidence in a text about the environment, culture and social situation

UK teenager launches sustainable fashion line

A resourceful teenager from the UK is taking sustainable fashion to the next level with designs he creates from things which most people would class as rubbish. Until a few months ago Joey Luciano did not even know the basics of

5 sewing. However, to combat boredom the 19-year-old learnt a new skill and created an entire wardrobe by upcycling second-hand clothes.

Joey Luciano

Before the Covid-19 pandemic hit in March 2020 Mr Luciano was studying Art and Design at college. His course, however,

10 was cut short and the teenager was not able to even complete his final project. Mr Luciano explained that like many others he felt "uninspired" and "unhappy" during lockdown. This is why he decided to learn a new skill. With only limited pattern cutting and sewing experience, he used YouTube tutorials to

15 teach himself. The art student started making one-of-a-kind T-shirts, jogging bottoms, shorts, tote bags and bucket hats using a sewing machine that he borrowed from his grandmother. The collection of garments are all made using colourful patches from clothes Mr Luciano had already purchased from second-

20 hand shops.

Glossary

upcycle reuse something to create a product of a higher standard

resourceful clever at finding ways of doing things

combat resist or try to stop something

entire whole or complete

baggy (clothing) loose and hanging in folds

Mr Luciano said he released all together nine garments on his website Lowr3s and almost all of them got sold out within the first 15 minutes. Recently the student also invested in an embroidery machine that he plans to use for any upcoming

25 projects. Mr Luciano described the style as "all-round DIY", "90s patchworks" and "quite baggy" and added that people of all ages can wear them, rather than just teenagers.

From Textile Value Chain

- Examine and discuss a wide range of texts
- Find evidence in a text about the environment, culture and social situation
- Adapt writing style and register for intended audience and purpose

Comprehension

1 What led Joey Luciano to make clothes with recycled fabrics?

2 What skills did Luciano need to make the garments, and what distinguishes them from traditional clothing manufacture?

3 How would you describe the style of Luciano's designs, and the intended wearers of his clothing range?

4 What new piece of equipment has Luciano purchased, and what kinds of design possibilities does it introduce?

1 Which compound word signals that these garments are individually created, and not intended for mass manufacture?

2 What associations does the word 'upcycle' communicate, and how is it related, but different, to 'recycle'?

1 What do you think of Luciano's fashion solution for reusing and upcycling low-quality fabric and clothing remnants?

What problems might be associated with 'fast fashion'? Do we have a responsibility to make ethical choices when we choose what to wear?

Writing a brief for an upcycled design label

Working with a partner, come up with a 'do-it-yourself' clothing or accessories line with a difference. Write a proposal outlining your plan to recycle or upcycle existing styles and materials.

- Do some research into the latest innovations in recycling and reuse, looking at new ways to upcycle or recycle clothing and other consumer waste products.
- Think about how you will source and make use of existing materials and styles to put together a new product line. What is the look you are trying to achieve?
- Identify what is unique about your business model, who you think your fashion and/or accessories line will most appeal to, and how you can reach out to them.

Share your plan with another pair and offer each other feedback.

Language tip
Words with the prefix *up-* are often used to show progress, positive change or moving higher.

For example: 'upcycle', 'upgrade', 'uplifted'.

A popular new shop

This translated text by the nineteenth-century French novelist Émile Zola is the first major work of fiction to focus on a department store. The 'Ladies' Paradise' is the name of the department store and is also the title of the novel. Written from the point of view of a young woman called Denise, who has just arrived in Paris and is working in her uncle's store across the street, this extract is her eye-witness account of the dramatic first day of the opening of the Ladies' Paradise.

- Examine and discuss a wide range of texts
- Examine closely how texts mirror the time and place in which they are written

The shop windows

But what fascinated Denise was the Ladies' Paradise on the other side of the street, for she could see the shop windows through the open door. The
5 sky was still overcast, but the mildness brought by rain was warming the air in spite of the season; and in the clear light, dusted with sunshine, the great shop was coming to life, and business
10 was in full swing.

1880s Paris department store

Denise felt that she was watching a machine working at high pressure; its dynamism seemed to reach to the display windows themselves. They were no longer the cold windows she had seen in the morning; now they seemed
15 to be warm and vibrating with the activity within. A crowd was looking at them, a real mob made brutal by covetousness. And these passions in the street were giving life to the materials: the laces shivered, then drooped again, concealing the depths of the shop with an exciting air of mystery; even the lengths
20 of cloth, thick and square, were breathing, exuding a tempting odour, while the overcoats were throwing back their shoulders still more on the dummies, which were acquiring souls, and the huge velvet coat was billowing out, supple and warm, as if on shoulders of flesh and blood.

25 But the furnace-like heat with which the shop was ablaze came above all from the selling, from the bustle at the counters,

Language tip

Before the era of global travel and widespread photography, writers offered vibrant accounts of new experiences to their curious readers.
For this reason, nineteenth-century novels often include very detailed descriptions with exceptionally long sentences that were carefully crafted with a range of punctuation marks, including colons, semi-colons and many commas.

- Examine how a writer uses a variety of language and grammatical features
- Examine closely how texts mirror the time and place in which they are written
- Write using a variety of sentence structures for different purposes

which could be felt behind the walls. There was the continuous roar of the machine at work, of customers crowding into the departments, dazzled by the merchandise, then propelled
30 towards the cash-desk. And it was all regulated and organized with the remorselessness of a machine: the vast horde of women were as if caught in the wheels of an inevitable force.

From *The Ladies' Paradise* by ÉMILE ZOLA

Comprehension

1 What is the dominant industrial metaphor in the description of the shop? Find the key words and phrases that identify this.
2 Why are the customers described in the plural form? Find the key words and phrases that characterize them.
3 **a** The writer makes effective use of personification to describe the materials in the shop. Find four examples of this technique in the extract.
  b Describe the effects that are created by these examples.
4 What sense is created by the metaphor the writer uses in the final paragraph to describe the 'selling' and 'bustle' at the counters'? (lines 25–32)

1 What similarities do you think there might be between this description from 1883 and one written about a popular new shop opening today?
2 How do you think consumer culture has changed from the nineteenth century to today?

Glossary

mob large, often aggressive, crowd of people
covetousness state of wishing to have something that belongs to someone else
exude give off a feeling, moisture or smell
acquire get or be given something
horde large group or crowd
inevitable unavoidable; sure to happen

Visualizing the scene as a graphic novel

Rework this scene from Émile Zola's *The Ladies' Paradise* as a graphic novel.

- Roughly outline and storyboard the scene to represent the story as it is described.
- Come up with appropriately scripted spoken and non-verbal language (speech and thought bubbles).
- Set the novel in the time and place it is written (Paris in the 1880s) or, if you like, in a different time and place (as is often done in films adapted from historical novels).

Share your scene with a partner and compare your creative visions!

Demands of a fashionista

- Examine and discuss a wide range of texts
- Find evidence in a text about the environment, culture and social situation

In this extract from a trilogy of novels that began with *Crazy Rich Asians*, the Singapore-born American novelist Kevin Kwan writes about a fictional visit to the showroom of the Italian designer Giambattista Valli during Paris Fashion Week. In this extract, Valli's assistant Luka entertains a group of rich Singaporean clients that include the ultra-rich fashionista Kitty Bing.

Paris Fashion Week

Kitty glanced at the ball gowns that were being paraded before her, feeling a little bored. Yes, it was so beautiful, but after the tenth dress, it was all beginning to look the same. Was it possible to have
5 too much beauty? She could buy up the whole collection in her sleep and forget she ever owned any of it. She needed something more. [...]

Gustav Klimt's painting entitled *Adele Bloch-Bauer I*, painted 1903–1907

Luka recognized the look on Kitty's face. It was the same expression he had seen all too often in some of his most
10 privileged clients – these women who had constant, unlimited access to everything that their hearts ever desired – the heiresses, celebrities, and princesses that had sat in this very spot. He knew he needed to change direction, to shift the energy in the room in order to reinspire his high-spending client.

15 "Ladies, let me show you something very special that Giamba has been toiling away at for weeks. Come with me." He pressed against one panel of the boiserie walls, revealing Giambattista's inner sanctum – a hidden workroom that contained only one gown displayed on a mannequin in the middle of the pristine
20 space. "This dress was inspired by Gustav Klimt's *Adele Bloch-Bauer I*. Do you know the painting? It was purchased for $135 million by Ronald Lauder and hangs in
25 the Neue Galerie in New York."

Glossary

fashionista devoted follower of fashion
privileged advantaged person or group
inner sanctum private place where very few people are allowed to go

30 The ladies stared in disbelief at the artistry of the off-the-shoulder ball gown that transformed from ivory tulle at the bodice and into a shimmering gold column, with a cascading train-length skirt embroidered with thousands of gold chips, lapis lazuli, and precious gemstones, painstakingly scattered into a swirling mosaic pattern. It truly looked like a Klimt painting come to life.

"It's unbelievable!" Georgina squealed, running one of her long manicured nails over the gem-encrusted bodice.

35 "Ravissement!" Tatiana commented, mistakenly trying to show off her secondary-school French. "Combien?"

"We don't have a price on it yet. It's a special commission that's taken four full-time embroiderers three months to assemble so far, and we still have weeks of work to go. I would say that

40 this dress, with all the rose-gold disks and precious stones, will end up costing more than two and a half million euros."

Kitty stared at it, her heart suddenly beginning to pound in that delicious way it did whenever she saw something that aroused her. "I want it."

45 "Oh, Madame Bing, I'm so sorry, but this dress is already spoken for." Luka smiled at her apologetically.

"Well, make me another one. I mean another three, of course."

"I'm afraid we cannot make you this exact dress."

Kitty looked at him, not quite comprehending. "Oh, I'm sure
50 you can."

"Madame, I hope you will understand … Giamba would be happy to collaborate with you on another dress, in the same spirit, but we cannot replicate this one. This is a one-of-a-kind piece made for a special client of ours. She is from China

55 also—"

"I'm not from China, I'm from Singapore," Kitty declared.

"Who is this 'special client'?" Wandi demanded, her thick mane of Beyoncé-bronzed hair shaking indignantly.

"She's a friend of Giamba's, so I only know her by her first
60 name: Colette."

From Rich People Problems *by* KEVIN KWAN

- Find evidence in a text about the environment, culture and social situation
- Participate fully in discussions

Glossary

tulle silky net material used for veils, curtains and dresses

lapis lazuli blue rock containing lazurite, calcite and pyrite

encrusted covered with a crust or layer

replicate make an exact copy of something

Comprehension

1 How do you know Kitty usually gets what she wants?
2 How does Luka make a special effort to keep his clients inspired, and how does it backfire?

1 Find the quote within the quote in the extract, and identify the rules around single and double quotation marks.

1 What is your impression of Kitty Bing?
2 How can you tell that this writing is satirical? Look back to the 'Learning tip' on page 29 to help you.
3 Compare this piece of contemporary fiction about fashion with the extract on pages 189–190.